EFFECTIVE EXHIBIT INTERPRETATION AND DESIGN

EFFECTIVE EXHIBIT INTERPRETATION AND DESIGN

TESSA BRIDAL

A DIVISION OF ROWMAN & LITTLEFIELD
Lanham • Boulder • New York • Toronto • Plymouth, UK

ALTAMIRA
PRESS

Published by AltaMira Press
A division of Rowman & Littlefield
4501 Forbes Boulevard, Suite 200, Lanham, Maryland 20706
www.rowman.com

10 Thornbury Road, Plymouth PL6 7PP, United Kingdom

British Library Cataloguing in Publication Information Available

Library of Congress Cataloging-in-Publication Data

Bridal, Tessa, 1947-
  Effective exhibit interpretation and design / Tessa Bridal.
    pages cm
  Includes bibliographical references and index.
  ISBN 978-0-7591-2110-2 (cloth : alk. paper) -- ISBN 978-0-7591-2111-9 (pbk. : alk. paper) -- ISBN 978-0-7591-2112-6 (electronic) 1. Museum techniques. 2. Museum exhibits. I. Title.
  AM151.B75 2014
  069.4--dc23

                                                        2013030524

∞™ The paper used in this publication meets the minimum requirements of American National Standard for Information Sciences—Permanence of Paper for Printed Library Materials, ANSI/NISO Z39.48-1992.
Printed in the United States of America

table of contents

Acknowledgments

All of the institutions and individuals mentioned here represent the generosity of museum professionals. They shared unstintingly of their time, their resources, and what they have learned and discovered over decades of experience. I hope that this tribute to them and to their contributions to the field makes them proud.

In addition, my thanks go to the International Museum Theatre Alliance, and most particularly to its Board of Directors.

Thanks are also due to the Science Museum of Minnesota, the Children's Museum of Indianapolis, and the Monterey Bay Aquarium for the resources they shared, and the professional and life experiences they made possible for me during my time with them.

Sameen Ghazali worked closely with the collaborators to create, copy edit, and lay out an introduction for each featured institution; she also organized, tracked, maintained credits for, and helped to select photos. She organized the resources put at our disposal, and she maintained contact with the institutions collaborating with us, always cheerfully and with no more compensation than my heartfelt thanks. My deepest appreciation also goes to Kristen Molle, who on her own time helped me over the finish line and kept me sane with her calm, "can do" assurances. Completing this project without Joe Chiappa's technical and editing skills would have been impossible. For the hours he sat patiently with me, and for his and his wife, Cat's, generosity of spirit, I give more appreciation than I can express.

For putting me on the museum path, bearing with my steep learning curve, and most of all for believing I could do it, my abiding love and thanks to Sondra Quinn.

List of Figures

List of Abbreviations

American Alliance of Museums (AAM)

The Children's Museum of Atlanta (CMA)

Carpenter Science Theatre Company (CSTC)

The Minnesota History Center (MHC)

The Missouri History Museum (MHM)

The Minnesota Historical Society (MHS)

Museum of Science and Industry, Chicago (MSI)

The National Children's Museum (NCM)

The National Museum of American History (NMAH)

The Science Museum of Minnesota (SMM)

The Science Museum of Virginia (SMV)

The Museums

The Children's Museum of Atlanta (CMA)
Pamela Duncan, Manager of Museum Programming

- **Mission:** CMA's mission is to spark imagination and inspire discovery and learning for all children through the power of play.
- **History:** CMA began in 1988 as a virtual museum or a "Museum without Walls," providing programming, in collaboration with other organizations, to schools and nonprofit organizations. On March 1, 2003, in downtown Atlanta's Centennial Olympic Park, it opened a family-friendly space designed to spark discovery, creative thinking, and artistic expression. The Museum without Walls roots are kept alive through extensive outreach programs in underserved Atlanta neighborhoods. Programs and exhibits are designed for children under eight and their adult caregivers, with particular focus on ages two to five years.
- **Square footage:** 16,000 square feet
- **Demographics and attendance:** CMA receives over two hundred thousand Georgia visitors annually, as well as tourists from outside the state. Audience demographics are 42 percent African American, 44 percent Caucasian, 9 percent Hispanic, 5 percent Asian American, and less than 1 percent Native American. The demographics of the more than two thousand children served through the museum's outreach programs represent approximately 85 percent African American, 10.2 percent Caucasian, 3.3 percent Hispanic, 1.2 percent Asian American, and less than 0.2 percent multiracial.

- **Fun fact:** The CMA bus, called The Imagine It Express, is fueled by recycled French fry oil.

The Minnesota Historical Society (MHS)
Wendy Jones, Director, Lifelong Learning and Museum Education

- **Mission:** MHS's mission is to use the power of history to transform lives: preserving, sharing, connecting.
- **History:** Founded in 1849, MHS is the oldest institution in the state. It is a private, nonprofit educational and cultural institution, with over twenty-four thousand members, the largest of any state historical organization in the country. MHS collects, preserves, and tells the story of Minnesota's past at twenty-six museums and historic sites throughout the state by means of its educational programs and materials for schools; extensive collections; a major research library; and the Minnesota Historical Society Press. Its flagship museum, the Minnesota History Center (MHC), opened in 1992.
- **Square footage:** The 427,000-square-foot MHC is the headquarters for the Society's operations and is located in St. Paul's governmental and cultural corridor. The History Center contains 45,000 square feet of exhibit galleries.
- **Demographics and attendance:** More than 250,000 people visit MHC annually. The great majority of visitors (90 percent) are from Minnesota; 81 percent live in the seven-county metropolitan area. Minorities account for 10.6 percent of the state's population and about 24 percent of the metropolitan population. Just over 5 percent of History Center visitors report a minority background. Children, excluding those in school groups, accompany nearly half of museum visitors.
- **Fun fact:** The MHC is home to the nation's largest collection of underwear. Over five thousand square feet of storage space houses more than 3,500 undergarments, from corsets and panties to union suits and boxers. There's even a patriotic "stars and stripes" bra and girdle from World War II. The collection came to MHS when Munsingwear went out of business and donated its entire collection of product samples, dating back to the company's nineteenth-century origins as the Northwestern Knitting Company.

The Missouri History Museum (MHM)
Elizabeth Pickard, Assistant Director, Interpretive Programs

- **Mission:** MHM's mission is to deepen the understanding of past choices, present circumstances, and future possibilities; strengthen the bonds of the community; and facilitate solutions to common problems.
- **History:** The Missouri History Museum was established as the Missouri Historical Society in 1866. It was founded to rescue "from oblivion the early history of the city and the state." In 1913, it moved into Jefferson Memorial Building, constructed on the site of the entrance to the 1904 World's Fair. It was built with the proceeds of the Fair in memory of Thomas Jefferson and is the oldest memorial to Jefferson in the country. Subsidies allow MHM to offer free admission to the main exhibitions as well as hundreds of free programs. In 2000 MHM completed a ninety-two thousand square foot building expansion and renovation with the opening of the Emerson Center.
- **Square footage:** 129,000-square foot-Jefferson Memorial Building and Emerson Center, with 33,000 square feet of exhibit space. The separate Library and Research center is 104,000 square feet and houses archives and collections.
- **Demographics and attendance:** In 2011, MHM welcomed over 368,000 people—nearly a third of whom attended a program by the Community Education and Events Department (CEE), of which Interpretive Programs is a part. CEE presented over seven hundred programs in 2011. MHM serves a diverse audience, which is 35 percent African American.
- **Fun fact:** The museum owns and displays a replica of the *Spirit of St. Louis*, the plane Charles Lindbergh flew across the Atlantic in 1927. It was made by the same company and retrofitted to the exact dimensions of the original for the movie *The Spirit of St. Louis*. Legend has it that both Jimmy Stewart (the film's star) and Charles Lindbergh (a technical consultant for the film) flew the plane.

Museum of Science and Industry, Chicago (MSI)
Heather Barnes, Director of Guest Experiences

- **Mission:** MSI's mission is to inspire the inventive genius in everyone, and its vision is to inspire and motivate children to achieve their full potential in the fields of science, technology, medicine, and engineering.

- **History:** Established in 1933 and housed in the only remaining building from the 1893 World's Columbian Exposition, MSI was the first interactive museum in North America. MSI has welcomed more than 175 million guests to experience such iconic exhibits as the *Coal Mine*, the *U-505 Submarine*, and one-of-a-kind new exhibitions such as *Science Storms* and *YOU! The Experience*. Exhibits are complemented by more than sixty daily live science experiences. The Museum's Center for the Advancement of Science Education provides innovative programs that inspire thousands of inner-city youth to discover science through seventy after-school science clubs; improves classroom instruction and student achievement with courses for hundreds of public school science teachers; and changes teens' lives by empowering them with science knowledge, public-speaking skills, and college readiness.
- **Square footage:** MSI is the largest science museum of its kind in the Western Hemisphere, with nearly fourteen acres of exhibits and more than thirty-five thousand artifacts.
- **Demographics and attendance:** In 2011, attendance reached over 1.48 million. Nearly 1.5 million guests visit the museum each year, including more than 350,000 school children, making MSI the top field trip destination among Chicago-area zoos and museums.
- **Fun fact:** The first baby chick at MSI hatched in 1956.

The National Children's Museum (NCM)
Jillian Finkle, former Exhibit Developer/Program Manager: Theatre and Early Childhood
Robert Evans, Exhibit Developer/Special Projects Manager

- **Mission:** NCM's mission is to inspire children to care about and improve the world.
- **History:** From its incorporation in 1974 to early 1977, NCM was known as the Children's Museum of Inquiry and Discovery and operated as a "museum without walls." In 1979, the museum secured funding to purchase its first permanent home, a former convent and nursing home near Capitol Hill. It moved to the new location that same year and changed its name to Capital Children's Museum. In 2003, the U.S. Congress designated the organization to become the new National Children's Museum (NCM), and a year later the Capital Children's Museum facility was closed and the staff

began the process of designing and building a totally new museum. NCM opened its indoor experience at National Harbor, Maryland, in December 2012 and is scheduled to open its outdoor experience as funding becomes available.

- **Square footage:** NCM's indoor experience has eighteen thousand square feet of space, and the outdoor experience will have sixty thousand square feet of space.
- **Demographics and attendance:** Annual attendance in 2012 and the first quarter of 2013 has been over sixty thousand and is expected to reach 480,000 visitors annually, 75 percent of whom will be from the region. The museum is slated to serve a national constituency of children, including the over 1.2 million children living in the local community and the 17.7 million tourists who visit the Washington area each year.
- **Fun fact:** For many years the grounds of Capital Children's Museum was the home of a giant Cootie® bug. The fifteen-foot-tall sculpture based on the iconic children's toy was constructed in 1975 for a float in the Macy's Thanksgiving Day parade. It can now be seen at American Celebration on Parade at Shenandoah Caverns in Virginia.

The National Museum of American History (NMAH)
Christopher Wilson, Director of Daily Programs and African American History and Culture

- **Mission:** Through incomparable collections, rigorous research, and dynamic public outreach, the museum explores the infinite richness and complexity of American history. It helps people understand the past in order to make sense of the present and shape a more humane future.
- **History:** Nearly sixty years ago, on June 28, 1955, President Dwight D. Eisenhower signed a bill authorizing $36 million for the creation of a Museum of History and Technology. It opened to the public in January 1964 as the sixth Smithsonian building on the National Mall in Washington, D.C. Since then, four million visitors a year have passed through the doors to enjoy the museum's exhibitions, public programs, educational activities, collections, and research facilities. Millions more make virtual visits to the museum's website. In 1980, the museum's name was changed to the National Museum of American History to better represent its basic mission—the collection,

care, and study of objects that reflect the experience of the American people. The museum collects and preserves more than three million artifacts, from the original Star-Spangled Banner and Abraham Lincoln's top hat to Dizzy Gillespie's trumpet and Dorothy's ruby slippers from *The Wizard of Oz*. The museum's collections comprise the greatest single collection of American history.

- **Square footage:** Approximately 750,000 square feet
- **Demographics and attendance:** 4.63 million visitors (No demographics available.)
- **Fun fact:** In 2000, conservators snipped 1.7 million stitches from the linen backing that was damaging one of the museum's most iconic objects, the Star Spangled Banner.

The Science Museum of Minnesota (SMM)
Stephanie Long, Director of *Science Live*

- **Mission:** SMM's mission is to turn on the science: realizing the potential of policy makers, educators, and individuals to achieve full civic and economic participation in the world.
- **History:** Founded in 1907 as the Saint Paul Institute of Science and Letters, SMM welcomes nearly one million visitors each year to see its world–class collection of dinosaurs and fossils, the nation's only convertible IMAX Dome Omni Theater, its trademark hands–and bodies-on science exhibits, and a slate of traveling exhibitions. SMM has occupied several locations in its one-hundred-plus-year history, and it opened its current facility in 1999. Moving the facility involved transporting 1.75 million artifacts and specimens, including a 3,900-pound iguana sculpture made of railroad spikes on an open semi flatbed. SMM is the most visited museum in the five-state region.
- **Square footage:** SMM is based in a 370,000 square foot facility.
- **Demographics and attendance:** Annual attendance is more than seven hundred thousand visitors. Attendance for fiscal year 2011 (June 1, 2010–June 30, 2011) was 796,000. About 63 percent of visitors are female, 90 percent of visitors are ethnically white, 45 percent of visitors use science in their daily work, and 43 percent have a college degree. About 55 percent of group composition is made up of adults and children.
- **Fun fact:** In addition to being the leading museum producer of large-format IMAX films, SMM is also one of a group of organizations that creates and distributes museum exhibits to an international market and custom builds exhibits for museums across

the country. SMM is a pioneer in the museum industry in its use of theatre as an interpretive tool. Founded in 1971, the *Science Live* Theatre program celebrated its forty-first season in 2011.

The Science Museum of Virginia (SMV)
Larry Gard, Artistic Director, Carpenter Science Theatre Company (CSTC)

- **Mission:** SMV's mission is to inspire Virginians to enrich their lives through science.
- **History:** On July 1, 1970, the Virginia General Assembly passed legislation that gave birth to the Science Museum of Virginia. Friends of the museum pressed the state to allow the museum to move into part of the old Broad Street Station, built in 1917 and destined for the wrecking ball. The museum's staff occupied Broad Street Station on January 22, 1976, and its first exhibit gallery was dedicated a year later, the culmination of over seventy years of effort to establish the Science Museum of Virginia. As of 2011, the museum houses a number of permanent and traveling exhibits throughout Broad Street Station as well as at two satellite locations. It also houses a theatre company, a thirty-ton moveable kugel ball, a Foucault pendulum, *Science on a Sphere*, and a variety of live animals—including their own rat basketball team. Their IMAX® Dome is the largest screen in Virginia.
- **Square footage:** Approximately eighty-thousand square feet of exhibit space at the museum's main location at the Broad Street Station, and two satellite locations: the Virginia Aviation Museum and the Danville Science Center.
- **Demographics and attendance:** Annual attendance for 2011 was 191,000. About 80 percent of visitation is from metro Richmond. The other 20 percent is composed of guests from the Virginia locations of Fredericksburg, Spotsylvania, and Williamsburg. Less than 3 percent of visitors come from outside Virginia. Of all admission sales, 30 percent is to school groups, and the rest is predominantly to families. In addition, the general admission audience is 75 percent female.
- **Fun fact:** The historic Broad Street Station in Richmond, Virginia, which is the home of the SMV, was designed by the architect John Russell Pope in 1917. Mr. Pope also designed the Thomas Jefferson Memorial, Constitution Hall, and the National Archives building in Washington, D.C.

Introduction

When I transferred almost three decades ago from the world of live performance to the world of museums, I was surprised to discover how similar, and at the same time how different, the production of a play and its design is to the process of exhibit development. One of the big differences I soon discovered was that, unlike stage sets, exhibits are expected to tell the whole story through a variety of mediums, such as labels, dioramas, artifacts, and electronic media.

I was tasked with adding live interpretation to exhibits, and it was my theatre background that interested my employers, in spite of the fact that one of the curators had made it clear that he would only tolerate theatrical interpretation so long as "the circus" came nowhere near *his* gallery. I have since come across this attitude expressed as concern over the aesthetic of an exhibit, an aesthetic that would be not only compromised but also "Disneyfied" by the presence of certain kinds of interpretation and interpreters, namely actors, especially actors in costumes, and puppets. There are a wide variety of opinions about the influence of Disney and theme parks on museums: from needing to model ourselves after them before we became obsolete to avoiding the model at all costs lest the fantasy and carefree entertainment they subscribe to should trivialize and compromise us.

This book describes the rich menu of interpretive offerings available to us, how we can benefit from live interpretation without compromising our overall style, and what a parallel exhibit design and interpretation development process should include in order for interpretation to be as thoughtfully and thoroughly planned as the exhibit itself. Also included are explanations of the plethora of terms used by the field, a proposed organization of those terms, and standards and best practices designed to inform interpreters and exhibit designers alike.

As I initially experienced live interpretation, it was as an enhancement, an add-on, icing on the cake—delicious, but not strictly necessary—since effective exhibits were designed to stand alone.

It was rare thirty years ago to find an interpreter included in *any* of the exhibit planning phases, let alone the early ones that might have contributed to the design of spaces and the placement of exhibit components that would allow for live interpretation. As time went by and interpretation programs grew in popularity, so did the plethora of terms describing the spectrum of offerings, and what visitors, and the field, can expect from them: terms such as *museum theatre, demonstrations, facilitated programs, storytelling, character appearances, informal interpretation, scripted programs, improvisational programs, creative dramatics, exhibit hosts,* and *first person.* According to who is using them, these terms mean different things to different practitioners, and they go a long way toward explaining why there is confusion about methods and styles.

When I was hired by the Science Museum of Minnesota, the museum had a thriving slate of science demonstrations and was interested in reviving a successful experiment with theatre that had been discontinued only because of lack of funds. Funding had been restored, and the museum had created two departments—a theatre department and a demonstration department working side by side, often competing for resources and audiences, with next to no participation in exhibit planning and little communication museumwide regarding why, when, and how new programs should be developed and scheduled.

Being an organization open to changes that would maximize resources and lead to more effective communication, the museum accepted my proposal to merge theatre and demonstrations into a single public programs department that would produce museum theatre pieces and science demonstrations, allowing for the use of theatrical techniques in both, as appropriate. Core teams integrating designers and educators, and including interpreters, soon followed.

In 1985, under the guidance of Sondra Quinn,[1] I organized the first annual Theatre in Museums Workshop. It has since been attended by national and international institutions, including art, children's, history and natural history museums, aquaria, and zoos, providing me with an opportunity of learning why these institutions were seeking training in theatre and the use of theatrical techniques. I've concluded that:

- Institutions seek proven educational and entertainment methodologies with which to engage their audiences in the messages of their exhibits, and inspiring visitors to encounter and wrestle with the ideas supporting those messages.
- Most educators and interpreters are not included in or empowered to influence the exhibit design process in order to plan for effective programming in exhibit spaces.
- Institutions have few available resources to assist them in understanding the spectrum of interpretive offerings and how interpretation can benefit them.

As the *Journal of Museum Education*[2] pointed out in 2008, "departments responsible for interpretation and public programming have been impacted profoundly" by the need to design and "facilitate dynamic, dialogic experiences that will ignite visitors' imaginations, ideas, and emotions and encourage self-reflection and social engagement" and by how "these new priorities require new expertise, organizational structures, and roles."

Great strides have been made in determining national standards and best practices for museums and for elements of their work, such as collections. For interpretation we can refer to the Characteristics of Excellence for U.S. Museums[3] (American Association of Museums, now the American Alliance of Museums) and to AAM's Interpretation and Education Information Center Fact Sheets, which summarize a National Interpretive Planning Colloquium held in May of 2005.

In 2003 and 2004 the American Association of Museums considered the possible addition of institutionwide interpretive plans as part of the accreditation process. A task force developed a working definition of a Comprehensive Interpretive Plan, but currently AAM does not require either an education or an interpretation plan for accreditation. As the recognition grows that including a live component to exhibit design is beneficial and attractive to audiences, this is bound to change.

The term *interpretation* covers label copy, exhibits, dioramas, and electronic media. In this book, it will be used to mean *live* interpretation.

The museums recognized below generously agreed to share their histories, collaborative exhibit development and interpretation processes, and the challenges they face in carrying those processes to fruition.

The Children's Museum of Atlanta (CMA)
Minnesota History Center (MHC)
The Missouri History Museum (MHM)
Museum of Science and Industry, Chicago (MSI)

National Children's Museum (NCM)
The National Museum of American History (NMAH)
The Science Museum of Minnesota (SMM)
The Science Museum of Virginia (SMV)

Notes

1. Sondra Quinn introduced the Science Museum of Minnesota to the blend of education and theatre that came to be known as museum theatre.

2. Jennifer Wild Czajkowski and Shiralee Hudson Hill, "Transformation and Interpretation: What Is the Museum Educator's Role?, *The Journal of Museum Education* 33, no. 3 (Fall 2008): 255–63.

3. American Alliance of Museums, Characteristics of Excellence for U.S. Museums, http://www.aam-us.org/resources/ethics-standards-and-best-practices/characteristics-of-excellence-for-u-s-museums. "The museum's interpretive content is based on appropriate research. The museum demonstrates consistent high quality in its interpretive activities. The museum assesses the effectiveness of its interpretive activities and uses those results."

As the American Alliance of Museums's (AAM) Standing Professional Committees Council tells us, "exhibitions are the public face of museums. The effective presentation of collections and information in exhibitions is an activity unique to museums, and it is through their exhibitions that the vast majority of people know museums."

The premise of this book is that the interpreters who bring these exhibitions—an institution's mission, collections, and stories—to life and to the forefront of a visitor's attention are an equally vital part of an institution's public face, and neglecting to give interpretation an equal seat at the table impoverishes the ultimate visitor experience.

That museums should give more attention and resources to exhibitions than to the means of interpreting them to the public is understandable given the foundational importance of exhibits to the very existence of museums. The premise of this book is that if they continue to do so it will be detrimental to their missions and affect their attendance.

This chapter will examine the outcomes of approaching exhibit and live interpretation design and development collaboratively, the challenges of adding interpretation to spaces and exhibits not designed for it, and the guiding practices put into place by some of the institutions who participated in this study.

These institutions were selected for their commitment to interpretation, their thoughtful and inclusive approach to it, and their desire to share what they have learned and experienced.

They describe their approach to exhibitions as a desire to develop exhibits that are educational, engaging, family friendly, and timely, or in some cases, timeless. They also want to make exhibits comfortable, engaging, and meaningful for their visitors, and they have found that it is here that interpretation can prove invaluable. As developers consider the learning styles, age, and cultural background of their audience, they can begin to build visual, auditory, and sensory experiences, along with the human interactions that will help visitors of all ages to make the connections and understand the underlying messages of each exhibit.

It is now rare to find institutions that don't use a team approach to exhibit planning. Most teams include exhibit designers, curators or content specialists, and educators. Some incorporate marketing, membership, volunteers, security, and operations. Some are organized into extended and core teams, ensuring that all team members have an opportunity to participate without having to attend every meeting. Others plan their agendas to focus periodically on the needs of different work groups.

I have found the most effective exhibit planning projects to be those that had core and extended teams, strong leadership, and team involvement on every level of decision making. In other words, members of the core team were expected to review exhibit, graphic, and interpretive plans and influence them. Education, for example, might identify a need for space or storage, or influence label design; designers would help identify aspects of the exhibit that needed live interpretation. On teams where each team specialist focused only on his or her specialty, fewer ideas were generated, and aspects of the guest experience were inevitably ignored.

When the Minnesota History Center (MHC) opened in 1992, it was with a new vision for history museums and exhibits that was informed by extensive audience research on how people connect with history and how people learn in museums. Barbara Franco, assistant director for museums in 1992, wrote:

> There has been a clear shift away from static exhibits that are expert-oriented displays of images, artifacts, and information, to programs that are more complex and open-ended, that actively respond to audiences' needs and varying learning styles, and are more akin to a two-way conversation with the visitor . . . The interpretive components in the gallery are not special add-ons . . . [T]hey are integral parts of the total exhibition experience designed to encourage choice, participation, and personal involvement.[1]

Wendy Jones, director of Lifelong Learning and Museum Education, was charged with "developing a menu of live interpretive programs that would meet visitors' diverse learning styles, extend and enhance exhibit content and themes, and function as a 'choice' for visitors in an environment of many other learning opportunities."

The MHC now makes it standard practice to include interpreter feedback sessions throughout the design process of both the exhibits and the programs, a change Jones credits to the wealth of firsthand knowledge interpreters bring to the table regarding how exhibits and programs work with diverse audiences. "No one spends as much time in the exhibits as our interpreters," she says. Their input in designing program spaces, interactives, and the programs themselves is considered invaluable, and exhibit designers make it a regular practice not only to see interpreters in action but also to solicit their advice on how different aspects of the exhibits are working. A member of the interpretive staff always consults with the designer about planned interpretive programs and space within the gallery. If there is no space, conversations still take place with curators about content or stories that could be told elsewhere.

It is expected of museums that they will have written standards and processes for exhibition design and development. These can include accessibility, accuracy, use of original and real artifacts, environmental considerations, funding guidelines, market appeal, regional relevance, and novelty.[2]

The Chicago Museum of Science and Industry (MSI) depends on the application of the "family-friendly exhibits" characteristics as described in *Family Learning in Museums: The PISEC Perspective*. These characteristics are that a family-friendly exhibit be:

- multisided—the family can cluster around the exhibit
- multiuser—interaction allows for several sets of hands and bodies
- accessible—the exhibit can be comfortably used by children and adults
- multioutcome—observation and interaction are sufficiently complex to foster group discussion
- multimodal—the activity appeals to different learning styles and levels of knowledge
- readable—text is arranged in easily understood segments
- relevant—the exhibit provides cognitive links to visitors' existing knowledge and experience[3]

MSI implemented a project team process that integrates staff from two distinct, but collaborative, divisions in the museum—Exhibits and Collections and Education and Guest Experiences—developing a core statement of purpose and a core message that provides a touchstone for the entire team, paying rigorous attention to the accuracy and relevancy of the content. MSI also follows a prototyping process for each exhibit, starting with simple models and narrative descriptions.

This approach has been successful in many ways, including extending on-going collaboration between the two divisions and leveraging high-quality exhibition content for multiple educational program offerings both within and beyond those exhibitions. This integrated process also facilitated the design of spaces.

When this process started, it was envisioned that the education coordinator would serve as a bridge to both student and public programming staff. Moving forward, it is more likely, Heather Barnes, director of Guest Experiences, says, that "individuals from *both* the student experiences/teacher programs teams and the guest experiences department will be brought into the exhibition team, as the design needs, goals and objectives for these different audiences are sufficiently different to warrant each group's direct participation."

While the initial approach necessitated some changes postexhibition opening, the collaborations initiated at the beginning of the projects continue to this day. This open dialogue allows MSI to optimize the delivery of programs for their varied audiences. As they move forward, MSI is considering the inclusion on the design team of someone with experience working with guests.

At the Missouri History Museum, interpretation is part of a larger department called Community Education and Events (CEE). Elizabeth Pickard, assistant director of CEE, who believes that programming is "a crucial part of the exhibition experience," shared that "collaboration with exhibit design in integrating performances into the galleries got off to a rocky start." Similarly, MHC experienced a less-than-successful exhibit and programs collaboration for their *Communities* exhibit when Education staff was facing the pressures of running a new museum and was minimally involved in exhibit planning. It took time and effort to figure out how to keep an educator on the team while running programs simultaneously, and how to develop the program and exhibit content in a way that they supported one other. In MHM's case the relationship between exhibitions, research, and theatrical interpretation was strengthened after Pickard served as a content curator for two exhibitions, making collaboration "a standard part of the process." At MHC Jones identifies collaboration as a pivotal moment during the development of the *Families* exhibit in the mid-1990s. (Addressed in "Challenges and Benefits," below).

These and other institutions that have moved to an integrated team approach to exhibit and interpretation development agree that aligning exhibit design and interpretation development processes in a way that meets the needs of both requires forethought, cooperation, and a flexible approach.

The National Children's Museum (NCM) incorporated live interpretation into the planning for a new museum from the start by designing exhibits that would accommodate it and by providing for a large, multipurpose theatre space and at least one smaller theatre for an in-house theatrical troupe.

At the Science Museum of Minnesota (SMM), one of their goals is to "provide audiences with accurate, up to date information presented in quality programs that reflect the best in entertainment and education." The museum has a long history with live interpretation, including floor staff that provides "pocket science" impromptu exchanges with visitors, a theatre company, and over three hundred volunteers who interpret content at activity stations throughout the main galleries and special exhibits.

MHM's exhibition design process is strongly team driven, and members of the CEE department are assigned as key personnel to each exhibition's team. CEE staff is especially valued because they have daily, frequent interactions with visitors and opportunities to observe how the public reacts to exhibition elements and experiences. Further, K–12, youth and family, adult, and theatre programs offer the exhibition team the opportunity to explore themes, topics, or ideas more deeply than is possible by electronic or written means. Early inclusion in the team process makes the finished interpretation programming a seamless part of the exhibit whole. Theatre at MHM most often focuses "on stories and people not well portrayed through exhibition content (objects small or non-existent, story of person tangential to the main exhibition narrative, etc.)." It is important to find those places where a human connection is most meaningful, and Pickard gave topics such as slavery or racial perceptions as examples.

These institutions have found that interpretation enriches the visitor experience, allowing them to:

- explore themes for which there is no space in the exhibit or which are difficult to display
- appeal to learners younger or older than the exhibit targets
- personalize the information in ways the exhibit itself may not be equipped to do
- add new programmatic elements to long-running exhibits and to keep the content up to date.

As exhibitions are a museum's public face, interpretation is its most open, accessible, and personal one, making exhibits more exciting by providing a variety of educational and emotional experiences.

Exhibit and Interpretation designers working collaboratively tend to find themselves in one of three situations:

- designing an exhibit and a program space, or spaces, *simultaneously*
- *retrofitting* an existing exhibit to accommodate a program space
- adding programs to existing exhibits with *no program space* included.

Designing an Exhibit and a Program Space Simultaneously

Exhibits that include program spaces from the outset can more easily have interpretation developed for them in the earlier stages of exhibit development. An example of this is the Children's Museum of Indianapolis's *Power of Children* exhibit, featuring the lives of three children—Anne Frank, Ruby Bridges, and Ryan White. The exhibit was designed to include three spaces representative of these children's lives: the Annex in Amsterdam where Anne and her family lived for two years in hiding from the Nazis; the classroom at William Franz Elementary School in New Orleans where Ruby Bridges was the first child to break the color barrier; and Ryan White's bedroom in Indianapolis, where his family moved after encountering prejudice when Ryan contracted AIDS. The bedroom includes items donated to the museum by Ryan's mother.

These three spaces are self-contained within the exhibit, with lighting and sound systems and doors that shut during presentations. At other times, multimedia shows are offered and the doors left open.

From the beginning, it was clear that these spaces would include presentations, and each was designed to accommodate a backstage area where actors prepare to make their entrances and where props and costumes can be stored. It was also clear that the interpretation department was charged with developing scripts that either included an appearance by the title characters themselves or told their story through one of their friends, family members, or helpers.

The picture below is of the Anne Frank portion of the *Power of Children* exhibit. With the exception of the benches, this is how the space looks at times when there are no performances. Otto Frank's wishes were that the Annex not be restored to how it was during the years that he, his family, and friends hid there, but rather that it be left as empty as he found it when he returned. The Children's Museum honored his wishes in its reproduction, including only a small table with a copy of Anne's diary on it.

Figure 1.1   Anne Frank Exhibit, *Power of Children*, Children's Museum of Indianapolis

Larry Gard, artistic director of the Carpenter Science Theatre Company at the Science Museum of Virginia (SMV), agrees that concurrent design of exhibits and program spaces is the most desirable way to go. At the same time, he acknowledges that "it is not unusual for designs to change according to space issues, availability of objects, funding, disagreements, delayed decision making, staffing, last minute changes brought about by outside influences (contractors, and others involved in the final product) and, not to be overlooked, the impact on the process of the personalities involved." At least one of the challenges Gard lists will be experienced by everyone working collaboratively.

I had an opportunity to deal with all of them concurrently in connection with an exhibit and its accompanying programs. From the outset it was clear to the core team (which included both exhibit and interpretation staff) that a small exhibit focusing on a number of different time periods and cultures, with large and small, real and reproduced artifacts, multimedia presentations, music, a variety of noisy interactives, and live programming expected to provide a living history feel, would present difficulties that were, if not insurmountable, as close to it as any of the team members had experienced. In addition, this exhibit involved complex technology that from the outset didn't work as planned and had to be redone. Two days before the exhibit was scheduled to open, the actors had only been able to rehearse in the exhibit during construction. Like many of life's lessons, this excruciating experience was also a learning one.

In effective exhibit and interpretation development processes, decisions about interpretation are made early in the process once the style of interpretive programming (e.g., theatrical, a science demonstration, informal interactions) has been decided, allowing for the planing and design of program spaces with adequate lighting, sound control, and seating.

In these cases, outlines and scripts may be presented along with exhibit elements for approval (e.g., *The Power of Children* referenced above). When approval is received, further development and implementation can proceed. In cases in which an interpretive space is considered desirable, even expected, but the style of interpretation hasn't yet become clear, it's advisable to allow that style to emerge along with exhibit content and design and a determination of what aspects of the content need enhancement or clarification. It isn't unusual for this to remain unclear until quite far along in the process.

In an ideal scenario, programs and exhibits receive equal attention and consideration, although not necessarily at every, or the same, phase of development.

At MHC, Jones believes that in the case of museum theatre, which she believes "extends, enhances, and illuminates exhibit content and themes," when a piece is developed for a specific exhibit, "its power is magnified (or diminished) by the setting in which it is performed. If the setting supports exhibit and program themes, the performance itself is energized. If the setting detracts from exhibit and program themes, the performance has to work twice as hard to create that energy between exhibit, program, and audience. Theater is most powerful when the content of the script, the design of the space, and the themes of the exhibit all support one another."

Retrofitting and Adding Interpretation to Existing Exhibits

The National Museum of American History's (NMAH) *We Shall Overcome* is an example of an existing small exhibit in a central location of Flag Hall to which a program with a big impact was added.

Flag Hall, planned during the museum's renovation to be a "Town Square" at the heart of the museum, became more of an interchange space for visitors crossing east to west in the museum. Due to poor acoustics and difficult traffic patterns, many of the programs originally intended for the space proved undesirable, and the daily programs staff found others that took advantage of the Hall's dynamics. One of its most popular is the flag-folding program, presented by a team of facilitators, educators, and interns, leading visitors in the folding of a replica of the 30′ x 42′ flag that flew over Fort McHenry in the War of 1812 and inspired "The Star Spangled Banner."

Wilson describes the program as giving "visitors a chance for a tactile experience with a flag the same size as one of NMAH's most iconic objects" and also taking advantage of the space "to produce a 'flash mob'-style program in which hundreds of visitors create a community in the Museum for 10 or 15 minutes, including singing the national anthem." This program was the result of experimentation in the space over several years in which staff evaluated what worked and what did not, until they found a model that achieved success.

Between March and August of 2005, after participating in a theatre program, more than seventeen thousand people joined hands near a display case containing objects from the Voting Rights March of 1965, including the coat worn by march leader Reverend Hosea Williams, which was torn during the violent attack on the marchers on Bloody Sunday, as well as his wife's, Juanita Williams, shoes, worn during the fifty-four-mile trek to Montgomery. Together, visitors gathered to sing the anthem of the civil

Figure 1.2   Flag Folding, National Museum of American History

rights movement, "We Shall Overcome," in commemoration of the for-
tieth anniversary of this historical event.

The thirty-minute dramatic and musical experience interpreting the
case used music and historical photos to share the stories and songs of civil
rights activists during their struggle for voting rights in Selma, Alabama,
culminating in a series of marches. The goal of the program was to present
the story in an engaging way for the large, walk-in audiences that visit the
museum in the busy spring and summer seasons, especially young visitors
coming to the Mall with their schools and families.

NMAH made it possible for visitors to contribute their thoughts after
the performance, which garnered overwhelming support for the program
from visitors who had themselves participated in the marches, as well as
from middle school children (one of the target audiences).

One of the program elements challenged visitors to respond to the
question "40 years after the Voting Rights Act, do you think that Americans still face obstacles to voting today?"[4] Participation was active, and
responses were posted on Talk Back Boards beside the stage, creating "a
lively discussion board where many different opinions were shared."

NMAH followed on the success of its *We Shall Overcome* program with
another program on the subject of civil rights that similarly expanded the
effect of an existing museum display. It was set at the whites-only F. W.
Woolworth lunch counter in Greensboro, North Carolina.

Join the Student Sit-Ins began in 2008 when the museum opened
after its two-year renovation. It cast visitors "as participants in a non-
violent protest training workshop a few weeks after the February 1,
1960, Greensboro lunch counter sit-in." Written and directed by Chris
Wilson, director of Daily Programs and African American History and
Culture, *Join the Student Sit-Ins* became a signature program for the museum, with more than 275,000 visitors participating in the performance
between 2008 and 2012.

Working in a building that hasn't been originally designed to accommodate either exhibits or performances presents unique challenges.
SMV is lodged in a historic train station, and staff is always searching
galleries for appropriate performance areas with adequate lighting,
where surrounding sounds won't be too much of a distraction and
where the flow of traffic won't be interrupted. In 2009 the exhibit
team, facilities team, and live interpretation staff came together and
decided to build a dedicated stage for both demonstrations and theatre
performances. Teamwork resulted in the mapping out of a location that
took into consideration:

- way-finding and visitor traffic
- audio-visual support (lighting, sound, wireless microphone)
- ambient distractions

A stage was built—with a raised floor approximately fifteen feet across by nine feet deep. A storage area for set pieces and props was constructed in the gallery wall. In addition, three large screens were included above the stage for highlighting details within a demonstration.

SMM has adapted its *Lava Live* demonstration, with a real lava pour, many times to meet various exhibit goals and needs. It was first created with a focus on Minnesota geology and had a successful run for decades in the *Our Minnesota* exhibit. When the museum designed and hosted the *Pompeii* exhibit, the show was adapted and moved into the touring exhibit space to deliver information about the Mount Vesuvius eruption. A room was designed in the exhibit as a performance space that also served as an art gallery of images of volcanic eruptions when the show was not being presented. Now in its third incarnation, *Lava Live*, condensed to five minutes, is performed outside the entrance to a temporary exhibit, *Nature Unleashed*. There was not sufficient room for the program in the exhibit hall itself, so knee walls were built outside the entrance to the exhibit, creating a temporary performance space with a sound system and graphics.

CMA added a program to its existing *Fundamentally Food* exhibit: *Eat a Georgia Rainbow*, a regular series of Sunday programs celebrating Georgia grown fruits, vegetables, and other crops featured according to the season. Imaginators, a group of professional actors and educators, guide children through a treasure hunt, storytelling program, and (cold) cooking activity. *Cooking with Colors* classes with a professional chef highlight the program on weekdays.

No Program Space

SMM's *Collections* gallery includes a sampling of objects from the museum's collections and offers a variety of programs, even though it does not contain a presentation space. Two examples of theatrical programs offered in the gallery are *The Spirit of the Mummy*, where costumes and props are designed to complement and expand existing exhibits, and *The World Puppet Theatre*, consisting of a small puppet stage that can easily be wheeled into the gallery.

The touring exhibit *Titanic* also did not include a performance space, so instead of presenting a show, actors portrayed the ship's crew, roaming the exhibit and chatting with visitors who had been given the recreated boarding passes of real *Titanic* passengers. This programming approach was so successful that SMM used it as a model for other exhibit programs, such as *Real Pirates* and *Lost Egypt*.

In 2007 CMA presented the Brooklyn Children's Museum touring exhibit *Night Journeys*. Its centerpiece was an oversized bed. Underneath it were drawers and toys that in the dark resembled monsters. CMA made the bed their set and seated the audience around it for their minimusical *It Happens at Night*.

MHC became expert at integrating cart activities into exhibit designs, ensuring that the activity relates to the surrounding exhibit themes and content, that a flat surface that looks like part of the environment is provided (e.g., a kitchen table in a kitchen setting, a picnic table in a backyard setting, a roll-top desk in an office setting) and with adjacent storage.

Challenges and Benefits of Collaborative Exhibit Design/Fabrication and Interpretation/Program Development

Communication

All participants identify communication as the most challenging issue and the biggest barrier to successful collaboration. Here we find all the challenges that plague human beings endeavoring to work together: we're territorial, defensive, inconsiderate, fearful, and judgmental to varying degrees; our tastes and cultures differ; as do our vocabularies and forms of expression. On the other hand, we are also generous, open, considerate, and courageous, and good leadership encourages and builds on these qualities.

Jones believes that an exhibit and its program space reflect the dynamics of the team that creates them.

> If the exhibit team is dysfunctional, the exhibit will be dysfunctional. Our worst program spaces were created by exhibit development teams that never found an effective means of working together. Our best exhibits, and best performance spaces, have been created by teams that cultivated the strengths, not the weaknesses, of individual team members.

The dynamics of a team are influenced, tested, strengthened, and stressed by factors including budget and space constraints, time (for designing, fabricating, collecting), and nonteam members with the authority to demand changes after plans have been approved. These changes can include redesign, and in the worst cases, refocusing of key content. This can reflect addressing errors, unforeseen circumstances, and at times institutional dysfunction, often in the form of micromanaging that permeates all levels of decision making.

The word *trust* comes up often at these times. Why have a team of experts in a variety of fields (design, interpretation, marketing, etc.) if they are not empowered to make decisions? Why are they often expected to incorporate changes when the developers do not consider the changes to be beneficial to the outcome?

This emphasizes the importance of ensuring that the style and vision for the project are clearly articulated by all those with the authority to make changes to it, and that strategic actions, such as including program development in each exhibit budget, are part of the process.

Another issue that frequently plagues collaborative projects is decisions made about changes to the design that don't take into account how the change will affect others using the space. Such issues can also be brought about by physical separation, within a building or buildings, of the various departments involved, which is a common challenge for larger institutions.

While all of the participating institutions speak enthusiastically about the benefits of an inclusive, collaborative approach, a common complaint is the time it takes for projects and programs to move forward, reach the approval stage, and move to the implementation phase.

Core and extended teams need access to the research informing the exhibit and program development and to be kept informed about updates to that research. (Technology can be useful here in the form of public and shared folders and drives.)

Budget decisions also need to be communicated and updated during team meetings, as do changes to exhibit design or components.

At MHC it took time and effort to find ways of developing new exhibits while simultaneously running existing ones. By the time the exhibit *Families* was being planned, the designer was receptive to feedback from interpreters, who by then had acquired experience working in exhibits. The designer facilitated feedback sessions with the interpreters during the exhibit development phase and ultimately changed the overall design based on this input. The performance space included presentations by History Players of Maud Hart Lovelace and Grey Cloud Woman, as well as short, multicharacter plays connected to exhibit themes such as "taking care" and "getting along." The History á la Cart spaces designer John Lindell created were seamlessly integrated into the design, and interpreters enjoyed working in them. "The environment," Jones says, "energized their interactions with the visitors, and their presence energized the overall exhibit design."

Jones goes on to explain that "because the live programs and the exhibit design worked so effectively together, the overall effect on the visitor was very powerful, as evidenced in the exhibit's summative evaluation.[5] I think that the exhibits we've developed that had weaker collaboration between exhibits and programs staff have had a 'duller' energy to them and have missed the mark in appealing to diverse audiences. Visitors are less engaged, less excited to be in that space, less likely to want to explore the space more deeply."

Barnes agrees, adding that "without strong, organized collaboration the end result has less chance of being cohesive and of serving the varied needs of the staff to develop and deliver quality programming, ultimately affecting the quality of the experience delivered to guests."

There is no question, as has been pointed out, that aligning exhibit design and program development processes in a way that meets the needs of both takes forethought, cooperation, and a flexible approach.

In order to assist communication and collaboration early in the planning process:

- Consider an institutional model that ensures that exhibits and interpretive programs are in close communication and full collaboration from the outset of the exhibit planning process.
- Identify a project leader.
- Determine individual and group responsibilities.
- Form core and extended teams. Core teams may include exhibits, education, guest experience departments, interpretation and public programs involved with all the details of the planning process, and they should meet more frequently than extended teams. Extended teams include the addition of departments that play important roles in support of the exhibit but may not need to be present at core team meetings (marketing, security, and retail, for example).
- Ensure that the head of programs is the mediator between outside programming contractors (playwright, director, costume designer) and exhibits.

MHC believes that an equal voice from all team members is essential. The exhibit is weaker when the educator does not have a strong voice. It is impossible to create effective program spaces when the people who must use them and make them resonate with visitors are not part of the development process.

Studies have shown that visitors who participate in programs spend more time in the exhibits. "Additionally," Amber Davis[6] tells us, "staff members (at the Denver Museum of Nature and Science)[7] observed visitors paying closer attention to the details of the dioramas after speaking with an enactor, and many visitors displayed critical thinking skills."

Organization

Meetings are a reality to be faced in the lives of most museum staff, and in the end, their effectiveness comes down to who leads them. It is up to that person to follow a few basic guidelines:

- Start and end on time.
- If you use an agenda—follow it.
- Give equal time to everyone with something to say about each agenda item.
- Stop the conversation whenever participants engage in "side conversations" with each other.
- Turn off your electronic devices and expect others to do the same.

These are fundamental requirements for establishing an atmosphere of respect and setting the ground rules for an effective meeting.

NCM recommends keeping detailed minutes from meetings, "with specific action items assigned to individuals."

Identify and agree on a streamlined and efficient decision-making process. It is essential that participants on a team be authorized to make decisions that drive the design and development process forward, staff understands each other's objectives, and roles and responsibilities are clearly defined.

Often, decision making is reduced to dates when people other than those serving on the team must give their approval. In a collaborative process:

- Clear direction is given about what each team member is empowered to do.
- A final decision maker is identified for the project.
- All team members have access to that decision maker.
- Opportunities are provided for conversation and discussion of differences as they arise.
- When using theatre and theatrical techniques with exhibit designers and developers who do not have a program development background, the head of programs is given an opportunity of going through every aspect of program production, rehearsal, and presentation.

- Decisions regarding interpretive programs (with the exception of content accuracy) lie with the interpretation program manager.

Time lines vary from department to department. A document outlining each department's deadlines is essential, accompanied by an early meeting during which departments address their needs and briefly describe why and when information, drawings, scripts, or approvals are essential before moving forward. Discussing the effects of delaying the process is also helpful for everyone to hear. This can avoid blame and negative evaluation and reviews of the process later.

In the case of interpretation programs, time lines need to include rehearsals held in the spaces where the interpretation will take place. Not enough importance is given to the need for interpreters to practice under circumstances as close as possible to those they will be encountering once the exhibit opens. It is not unusual for interpreters to be expected to practice with construction noise, dust and fumes, ongoing conversations and radio traffic, and with staff walking through the space.

Space

After communication, space is identified as the second biggest challenge facing exhibit and program planners.

How do we integrate the support that live programs need into the exhibit design? How do we provide enough storage and behind-the-scenes space? How do we make a program space interesting when no interpretation is taking place? Where do we put program spaces in the exhibit in a way that makes sense with the overall flow of traffic and visitor needs? (These questions surface for touring exhibits as well.)

Gard has observed the positive impact of live interpretation in a dedicated space, in SMV's case a stage fifteen feet by nine feet. It has contributed to an increase in the number of demonstrations and live theatre performances and to discussions as to whether SMV could dedicate more gallery space exclusively to live interpretation.

Dead Space

Designing multiuse spaces that can remain vital and engaging when live programs aren't being presented is highly desirable for designers of exhibits and programs alike.

A space designed for programs and performances that sits empty and unused when no programs are scheduled is described by Jones as a missed experience. This is particularly true when the space is set up with seating facing a stage, and the visitor perceives "that something should be going on there. If there is no indication that a program will happen soon, visitors feel that they have missed something, especially if the design of the space is not visually engaging."

MHC's first success in extending the design of exhibit content to the design of the performance space occurred in the *Manoominikewin: Stories of Wild Ricing* exhibit. Both the exhibit and performance space design drew heavily from the circle imagery in Anishinabe storytelling and the birch bark used so extensively in canoes and winnowing baskets used in the harvesting of wild rice.

Location

Program spaces need to be easy to locate. If they are in the rear of exhibits (away from the exhibit components intended to draw visitors in), signage about the program will be needed at the entrance. Hard-to-find spaces impact attendance at programs and lead to late arrivals; this in turn can make for late starts that create a domino effect on the schedule of performances and presentations.

Jones's wide experience with design leads her to state that

cul-de-sacs are bad—dead ends are dead ends. Don't design exhibits with lots of cul-de-sacs, and don't put the performance space in the center of the cul-de-sacs! In general, corner spaces work best. The visitor traffic flow created by a series of cul-de-sacs is both stifling for the exhibit's energy and problematic for performances. Think carefully about the flow of visitors throughout the entire exhibit when developing a performance space.

Spaces, Jones believes, dictate the style of programs that can be performed, which she describes as either "presentational or representational," adding that

you can't make powerful emotions resonate amidst chaos and distractions. It will be an uncomfortable experience for both the audience and the performer. Likewise, intimate spaces are overwhelmed by large, interactive experiences. These too can be uncomfortable for both the visitor and the performer.

Connection to Exhibit

Consider whether the program space needs to be adjacent or near to certain objects or exhibit elements. Rarely does the combination of interpretation and artifacts result in damage to either performers or artifacts. MHC, however, shared a hard lesson they learned. An artifact was mounted on the other side of a performance space where an actor's role called for slamming a door. Jones's recommendation: "Make sure adjacent artifacts are well-secured when you mix theater and exhibits!"

Sound and Activity from Adjacent Exhibits

Sound is no respecter of walls and barriers. When designing an exhibit's interpretation space, it's essential to keep in mind not only what surrounds the space but also the entire gallery. Separate noisy components from the interpretation space as much as possible, or give interpreters the means to turn those components off during programs.

MHM has installed on and off switches for sound and video elements in areas designated for performances. This has had "an enormous impact on the quality of the visitor experience."

Storage

Consider where set pieces, props, costumes, and equipment will be stored, and whether spaces can serve a dual purpose—programs and their props go in when activities or portable exhibit elements go out, and vice versa. Museums have stored materials in large, not very deep boxes that can be raised to ceiling level and lowered to the floor; behind closet doors that are integrated into exhibit walls; and in cabinets that double as activity stations.

A majority of SMM's theatre sets are on wheels, allowing actors to move sets and props from storage to the performance space.

Technical Needs

These include lighting, sound, microphones, props, and movable or immovable set pieces. In most museums, interpreters are expected to set up their programs and to clear them away when they're finished. This makes it essential to consider technical needs with sufficient time to design and build easily movable sets and props, and if lighting or sound are involved, to ensure that technical help is readily available before and during presentations.

Visitor Comfort

Planning ahead for expected attendance helps to prevent visitor frustration if the space becomes too crowded and visitors can neither see nor hear and are otherwise uncomfortable. Expect families to find places for their children to sit on the floor at the front, placing themselves at the rear. If they then decide to leave midprogram, they will retrieve their children, disturbing other audience members.

The only way to cut down significantly on the coming and going that makes museum presentations resemble street performances is to present programs in totally enclosed spaces and controlling attendance. This is recommended for presentations that require quiet moments or use the fourth wall.[8]

Providing some form of seating can also alleviate the problem, as can defining the space with lighting, the placement of sets, and curtains (these can be inset, like folding doors, and drawn only when a program is happening).

SMM immediately observed an increase in adult visitors watching shows when benches with back support were added to their atrium stage space.

Address the Needs of an Audience to See, Hear, and Focus

Basic as it may sound, there is little point in developing interpretation programs if the intended audience can't see, hear, or focus on the program with relative ease and comfort.

Seeing necessitates adequate lighting and an unobstructed view of the program for short and tall visitors alike. Will visitors stand or sit during

Figure 1.3   Cryogenics on the Atrium Stage, Science Museum of Minnesota

the program? The answer to this question often determines the length of the program. Seating can be provided for some, if not all, in the form of stools, benches, or even carpet squares. If seating is not an option, then the interpreter needs to feel comfortable taking charge of the space and moving people as needed to improve sight lines.

Hearing is often a bigger challenge than seeing. Hearing is not only a matter of sound reaching the ear in an audible manner. For the words you hear to have meaning you must be able to *focus* on them. In exhibits in which a barrage of sounds surrounds us, this is virtually impossible. Presenters need to be able to shut down surrounding media (video monitors, computer interactives, etc.) during a live presentation. When left on, media compete with the presentation and distract both visitors and performers.

Like media, interactives can be noisy and distracting during a live performance. Many interactives are low-tech, gross-motor-skill activities that are harder to "turn off" with the flip of a switch. Jones gives an example from one of the first exhibits the MHC opened, which included a squeaky oxcart wheel about ten feet away from the performance space.

> Visitors turned the wheel ad nauseum to make it squeak. Although its constant, high-pitched squeal did help all of us to empathize with the thousands of French Canadian, Métis, and other peoples who traveled the Red River Oxcart Trails between Winnipeg and St. Paul in the 19th century, it also created a significant amount of strife amongst staff and visitors alike. Since we couldn't just flip a switch to turn off the wheel during performances, we tried "shrouding" it in canvas during programs. But, of course, a little canvas never stopped a pack of 5th grade students from rooting out an opportunity to wreak havoc. We ended up abandoning the canvas and removed the wheel from the exhibit. We also learned that most noisy, low-tech inter-actives need to be far, far away from the performance space.

Examples

SMM's existing theatre was redesigned to be an object-automated show, a film space, and a live performance space, housing *Science on a Sphere*. To complement the exhibit *Future Earth*, a program called *Planet Earth Decision Theatre*, examining the impact humans have on the planet, was created for the theatre. The show uses I-Clicker remotes, allowing visitors to cast their vote about the future of our planet.

MHM uses in-gallery areas designed as gathering points for its regular theatre programming. These areas combine environmental, electronic, and standard exhibit elements (along with seating) that function both with and without performers in place. The exhibit about lunch counter protests

Figure 1.4   Planet Earth Decision Theatre, Science Museum of Minnesota

in St. Louis during the 1940s (similar to the protest program mentioned earlier in Greensboro) includes a reproduction lunch counter and stools. When there is no play going on, visitors can come up to the counter, sit, listen to audio interviews with protestors, and look at artifacts embedded in its top. When the play is going on, the lunch counter becomes the "set" and camp stools are brought in to accommodate the audience.

A similar idea is used at the Monterey Bay Aquarium as part of its *Seafood Watch* initiative. A lunch counter including stools is once more the focus, in this case with screens offering menu choices, and a video in the background of the exhibit featuring a chef and wait staff who comment on the choices made by visitors. The counter is designed for live interpretation, with room behind it for an actor to turn off the video and become one of the waiters. Printed menus are offered to the visitors, and props (such as a bucket of by-catch) are brought out to emphasize why certain choices are bad for the future of the oceans.

At MHM other spaces include moveable elements. For example, *Go Home Rosie!*, a large area about industrial work in St. Louis, becomes a performance space by bringing in stools and removing a hands-on model airplane activity station. In the Grand Hall, a small platform, chairs for the audience, and a flat are brought in to define the performance space. Archival images, props, and costumes are used to set the scene and mood, and audio cues can be played over the in-house sound system.

In its prior location, NCM designed exhibits to be immersive environments encouraging self-exploration and visitor-to-visitor interaction. While an informed staff person is considered essential to properly interpret the exhibit, provide context, motivate interaction and in-depth exploration, and facilitate a fuller understanding of the exhibits and their lessons, these immersive exhibits are designed to be stage sets in which the visitors become the actors and provide their own form of live interpretation.

As backdrops to the planned *My House to the White House*, NCM included a hometown campaign office and polling station, the White House, Supreme Court, and Capitol.

> As the exhibit design process progressed, the exhibit development staff began to envision the new Museum's exhibit experience as a form of theater with the visitor as part of the performance, with or without staff participation. The exhibits were to serve as stage sets with the visitors as actors in an unscripted, but guided performance. The audience would be encouraged to be an active, integral, and a key part of the exhibits, bringing them to life in a way that casual observers or disinterested bystanders would not do.

Bob Evans, Lead Exhibit Developer for *My House to the White House*, saw such exhibits as the embodiment of learning by doing. In *My House to the White House*,

> the visitor's journey begins by being fully immersed into experiencing the life of a regular citizen both at home and around town on a typical day in My Town (a day that just happens to be an election day) and ends with the visitor's elevation to the highest elected and appointed positions in American government in My Washington.

Jilian Finkle, formerly NCM's exhibit developer and program manager, adds that "rather than being just an enhancement to the *My House to the White House* exhibit, live public programs were envisioned as playing an integral and fundamental role in engaging children and challenging them." For example, the Town Square was designed for professional actors to portray candidates eliciting support from young voters through campaign speeches and improvised interactions in which they debated issues of specific interest to children, such as school uniforms, bike helmets, and whether wild animals should be allowed as pets.

After making and waving posters, cheering self-composed slogans, and voting, visitors would attend a victory parade and party in which the

Figure 1.5   Campaigners, National Children's Museum

results of the election were announced and the winning candidate made an acceptance speech. Following the oath of office, the program would culminate with a celebration complete with noisemakers, balloons, and even simulated fireworks.

Discuss the Various Styles of Interpretation Best Suited to the Goals of Your Exhibit

The first important consideration informing the collaboration between exhibit planning and interpretation is: *What kind of interpretation is needed and wanted in this exhibit, and what is the desired outcome?*[9] A description of interpretive styles and forms follows in chapter 2.

Results

What follow are positive outcomes resulting from the use of interpretation and close collaborations with exhibit developers and designers.

Keeping content current—Recognizing that programs can be updated and current events addressed more readily by interpreters than by modifications to labels or exhibit components has led exhibit designers and interpreters to collaborate on ways of updating content during the duration of exhibits. SMM has found that this ability to keep content current through interpretation draws returning visitors in to see what's new.

Guided learning—creating spaces that lend themselves to interpretation, and having an interpreter, facilitator, or scientist present, leads to the opportunity of answering questions, making personal connections for the visitors, and guiding them to other related exhibits.

The exhibit summative evaluations MHC has conducted over the years support the claim that live interpretation has a high impact on visitors.[10] MSI takes

> an intentional, research-based approach to developing and implementing live programming, using recent engagement literature findings, and making use of what is known about how individuals learn. . . . This approach places the visitor at the center of the engagement process, leveraging past knowledge, emotional connections and learning-by-doing.

Social engagement—Interpretation lends itself to creating experiences that encourage interaction not only with the exhibit and its interpreter but also among group members.

At MSI, the guest experience department underwent a significant transformation to position all guest experience staff to engage guests in museum and exhibit content with the launching of a *Science Rediscovered* campaign to help reinvent the guest experience, enhancing it by presenting a unique, dynamic visit that engages people in *interactive science experiences* that make learning fun and include improvisation and inquiry. The hiring, the training, and managing of staff was restructured to best position teams to engage guests in science content. Teams of scientists and facilitators also present interactive live science experiences. In each of these learning is based on a participatory and inquiry approach, with facilitators asking guests lots of questions and building on guest answers to tailor learning. Since launching this initiative the museum has increased the variety of *Live Science Experiences* and more than tripled the number offered on a daily basis at no additional cost to guests. It has also added to the number of facilitators positioned to engage informally throughout the museum, increasing the opportunities to make personal connections with guests, the number of people who engage in the content, and the number of positive guest comments. Guests note the overall positive impact facilitated experiences have had on their visit, from mentioning a specific learning point or a specific facilitator to an overall facilitated experience or live science theatre show.

Problem solving—Collaboration between departments at SMM led to the solution of how to prepare audiences for sensitive material in the *Dead Sea Scrolls—Words That Changed the World* exhibit. The exhibit focused on a collection of two-thousand-year-old documents, the earliest known copies of the Hebrew Bible. The exhibition also included the Saint John's Bible—the first complete Bible to be commissioned in five hundred years. Before visitors ever entered the exhibit, the museum wanted to address the reasons why a science institution would offer an exhibit dealing with religion. The planning team was concerned that a label might not be read by everyone, and that a video could be ignored, whereas a live presentation would require the audience to be more active listeners. The decision was made to design a confined space at the entrance to the exhibit, where a three-minute presentation was made by an interpreter. The outcome was that everyone entering the exhibit received the information considered essential by the museum. Visitor evaluations revealed that 65 percent of visitors felt that this style of delivery was more successful than a video. An equally desirable outcome was what Stephanie Long, director of *Science Live*, describes as "trust equity" between the exhibit, operations, and program team, which in turn led to future opportunities for interpretation and a bigger budget.

Creativity—Collaborative exhibit development often allows for thinking outside the box. The interplay of content, design, and audience can open up discussions about all the tools available for creating an engaging and provocative visitor experience. Jones maintains that it's not about one exhibit tool being better than another to engage visitors, but rather the effectiveness of the whole experience in order to make it memorable. "Too often," she says, "we pit interpretive tools against each other—the power of artifacts versus multimedia versus live interpretation—and museum departments see exhibit development as a battle for the supremacy of their particular interpretive focus."

Wilson believes that at the NMAH one of the benefits that resulted from collaboration also built trust among curators and administrators. The publicity garnered by *Join the Student Sit-Ins* in particular and the overwhelming support from visitors was persuasive, "but perhaps more than anything else, the experience of working closely together forged a strong working relationship between the curatorial and education staff that continued to grow."

At the SMM close to two hundred thousand people watch a *Science Live* show each year. *Science Live* reaches a wide range of visitors with approximately sixteen shows a year, focusing on a variety of scientific disciplines.

The museum finds that programs make content personally relevant and excel at stimulating a desire for further learning. As a side benefit to the community, consistent and rewarding work for theatre artists is provided, often introducing them to a largely unknown means of developing their craft.

Flexibility—By the early to mid-2000s, the NMAH was offering daily experiences that brought programming to where the visitors were. This represented a change in how the museum had offered programming in the past by taking into account how visitors used the museum. Typically, they came for short periods and then went on to another of the many attractions and monuments in Washington, D.C. This led the museum to determine that by the time the museum reopened from its major renovation in 2008, the number of times programs were offered would be increased, and that paid staff, including a new company of actors, would be used in addition to docents in the presentation of daily programs. They began by offering a daily theatre program, increasing the number of touch carts, turning the Hands-On Science Center into a new invention-themed *Spark! Lab*, and staffing the exhibition *Invention at Play* with facilitators. These changes saw the proportion of visitors engaged in conversation rise from 10 percent to more than 25 percent.

Notes

1. Barbara Franco, "New Audiences for an Old Institution: Using Exhibits to Expand the Educational Mission of the Minnesota Historical Society," *History News* 48, no. 5 (September–October 1993): 18–22.

2. The wisdom of having similar written standards and guidelines for interpretation is discussed in more detail in the next chapter.

3. M. Borun, J. Dritsas, J. I. Johnson, N. Peter, K. Wagner, K. Fadigan, A. Jangaard, E. Stroup, and A. Wenger, *Family Learning in Museums: The PISEC Perspective* (Philadelphia: The Franklin Institute, 1998).

4. A question that was still relevant in the presidential election of 2012.

5. Copies can be obtained by contacting Wendy Jones at wendy.jones@mnhs.org.

6. Amber Davis, "Findings," master's thesis, John F. Kennedy University, Museum Studies, 2013.

7. Kathleen Tinworth, manager, Visitor Research and Program Evaluation.

8. A theatre term describing the imaginary wall between the stage and the audience.

9. The reverse question—what exhibit does this interpretation need?—is rare. Two examples are: a) SMM's *Suitcase Science—The Science Behind People's Stuff*, where a team of actors conducted workshops collecting over three hundred stories about the science behind items owned by Minnesotans. The stories were

used to create a theatrical piece, a small exhibit component, and a book and an audio book distributed to libraries throughout Minnesota. Exhibit designers were given the monologues the actors wrote and turned them into exhibit copy. In other words, the programming inspired the design of the exhibit component and the exhibit copy. b) Atlanta Children's Museum's (ACM) *Under the Big Top!: Be Your Own Ringmaster* grew out of the very popular circus programming created by the Imaginators (interpreters). *Under the Big Top!* had "three rings" of activity exploring issues of physical fitness, health and nutrition, and self-image.

   10. Op. cit.

2

If collections are the heart of museums, what we have come to call education—the commitment to presenting objects and ideas in an informative and stimulating way—is the spirit.

—MUSEUMS FOR A NEW CENTURY COMMISSION REPORT[1]

As collections evolved from the private collector's cabinet to county, state, and federally supported institutions exhibiting a vast array of artifacts, so did the ways in which those collections were cared for, exhibited, and interpreted. Some of the greatest changes began during the second half of the twentieth century with the growth of science centers and children's museums, where collections were not typically at the core of such institutions' mission statements. They created exhibits that were regularly changed and updated, were interactive and hands on, and where visitors were encouraged to touch, play, and experiment in a way and to an extent that revolutionized visitor expectations and the culture of museums as a whole. Until that time, visiting a museum was a relatively passive event. Objects and dioramas were exhibited behind glass, there was no touching, and it was entirely up to the visitor to determine how many labels and panels of written information to read. It was unlikely that visitors would encounter someone who would "interpret" the objects and exhibits for them, let alone invite them to meet an actor portraying a spirit of the mummy, or to watch a scientific demonstration of alternative current.

This revolution extended to a remaking of the entire museum visit, transforming it into an experience, with the museum becoming a place where visitors could also shop, eat, and bring their children with the expec-

29

tation that there would be places devoted to them. A visitor could become a member, saving money on future visits, and also participate in the support of the institution, a role that until then had been limited to wealthy patrons and donors. Attracting visitors became essential, with departments created for that purpose and succeeding to such an extent that nowadays attendance at museums, zoos, aquaria, and historical sites exceeds that at sporting events.

Part of the attraction of these new and different museums became the opportunity to learn, and since education in and of itself can have negative connotations in North American culture, the *fun* of learning was emphasized, and words implying education were carefully selected. One of the ways in which these changes affected museums was the rise of departments that separated schools and education from public programs, at times leading to a heavy focus on the entertainment side of the educational mission.

These radical changes created, in the field of interpretation, a wide range of education and entertainment techniques and programs devised to engage visitors. Describing and defining these is the purpose of this chapter. These definitions are necessary to aid museums in communicating with one another, with funding agencies, and with our visitors; to clarify our own expectations of what these various programs can accomplish; and to establish standards.

Pickard describes interpretive programming as "the human interaction that occurs inside the galleries," with the focus being on a story and a conversation-driven approach with many hands-on opportunities and activities. This grows out of the National Park Service approach to interpretation laid out by Freeman Tilden in his 1957 book *Interpreting our Heritage*, where in his forthright way, he told us that "information is not interpretation, but all interpretation includes information" and that "interpretation that cannot connect the information to the visitor's own life experience is dead."[2]

When we look at the inventive names institutions have given to their programmatic offerings, it becomes clear why even the most knowledgeable interpretation practitioners have to ask for clarification when they talk to one another about their various programs. The resulting confusion and bewilderment in other areas of museum work, when speaking to those outside our field, or when applying for grants, is considerable.

A few examples of names given to educational and interpretive programs follow:

> Activities
> Celebrations
> Character Appearances
> Costumed Program Interpretation
> Creative Dramatics

Demonstrations
Education Workshops
Exhibit Hosts/Greeters
Facilitated Hands On
Facilitated Programs
Facilitated Role-Play
First Person
Gallery Theatre
Guest Presenters
Guided Exploration
Guided Tours
History á la Cart
History in our Hands
History Lessons
History Live
Informal Facilitated Activities
Informal Floor Activities
Interactive Learning Experiences
Learning Labs
Live Science Experiences
Mascots
Museum Theatre
Object Carts
Oral History
Performances
Presentations
Programs
Public Programs
Rhythm and Movement Activities
Science Demonstrations
Science Theatre
Scripted Demonstrations
Storytelling
Story Time
Street Theatre
Theatre
Touch Carts
Tours
Unscripted Demonstrations
Zone Work

Thirteen categories emerge from this wealth of choices. These categories and descriptions are intended as guidelines, with the understanding that two or more of them can be blended, as in examples of demonstrations that use theatrical techniques or roving characters that may also be exhibit hosts and greeters. These categories are not intended to replace descriptions already in place for an institution but to serve as a guide for placing those names in one of the thirteen categories at times when we need to communicate with entities outside our own institution.

Mascots

Iconic characters that represent the institution and are readily identified with it, mascots may appear on publicity materials and at museum events. They typically do not speak.

Examples

At TCM, Rex greets visitors at the beginning of the day and leads the end-of-the-day parade. Rex is performed by the museum's Actor Interpreters, all of whom are trained in Rex expectations: Rex is friendly, playful, welcoming, and energetic. He never "breaks character" by speaking or making movements and gestures not in keeping with his role as the museum's representative. He poses for photos with visitors. Whenever he is in a public area, he remains "in character."

He is the only mascot and the first of many characters that visitors will come across during their visit. His mission is to make visitors feel welcome and want to interact with him. Exposure to Rex prepares them for other interactions they may have with interpreters and actors throughout their time at the museum.

Similar to mascots are costumed characters that often accompany touring exhibits. CMA has had Arthur, Bob the Builder, Curious George, and Clifford the Big Red Dog. Cartoon characters often drive attendance and are very popular with younger visitors. CMA's Imaginators perform these, making movements and gestures germane to their character. Like mascots, they do not speak and are always accompanied by an Imaginator serving as a handler who verbally communicates for them.

In 2011 and through the spring of 2012, MHM hosted the Field Museum's traveling exhibition *Mammoths and Mastodons, Titans of the Ice Age.* They developed a seven-foot-long, six-foot-tall Mastodon puppet for a program centered on telling the difference between a Mammoth and a Mastodon. Based on suggestions from visitors and from Facebook fans, the puppet was named Meggie. Meggie became so popular that she soon

Figure 2.1   Rex/Interpreter, Children's Museum of Indianapolis

"took on a mascot role, making special photo opportunity appearances at member events, birthday parties and family program days. Even though the exhibit has now left, MHM plans to continue to use Meggie as a mascot for large family program days."

Figure 2.2   Meggie, Missouri History Museum

Exhibit Host/Greeter

A friendly, approachable, identifiable (by means of costuming or location) individual, who is knowledgeable about the exhibit and who can answer questions and make recommendations based on age and interest. The host/ greeter may wear a uniform, a costume reflecting the exhibit, and carry a prop connected to the exhibit. Host/greeters are typically stationed at the entrance to the exhibit. In some cases, the host/greeter may roam, engaging visitors, or lead visitors from the entrance to points of interest.

Examples

Stationed at the entrance to the exhibit, the Dora and Diego host at TCM carries an animal puppet connected to Diego's jungle adventures. The host greets visitors, shares animal facts, answers questions, and escorts visitors to points of interest within the exhibit.

MHC refers to similar work as Zone Work. Throughout the day, interpreters rotate through different "zones," which are usually one or more exhibits for which the interpreter is responsible. While in each zone, the interpreter has four primary functions: 1) to provide interpretive programming; 2) to facilitate the exhibit school program (school groups have self-guided activities provided by the MHC as a means of helping chaperones

Figure 2.3   Dora and Diego Host, Children's Museum of Indianapolis

navigate the museum); 3) to perceive and respond to visitors' needs and questions; and 4) to monitor the use of the exhibit.

Tours

This is a guided, group experience through all or parts of an institution, its exhibits, and behind the scenes.

Examples

At MHM gallery tours are provided to school and youth groups, as well as to adults. A corps of interpretive interns delivers the K–12 Gallery Classroom Programs. *Movement in Black and White* is one of these experiences, during which students make three station stops in the permanent galleries addressing the history of the civil rights movement in St. Louis. The classroom component is a dramatic movement workshop where students

Figure 2.4   Tours, Monterey Bay Aquarium

enact different civil rights movement experiences. For example, activist Ivory Perry used to block traffic to bring attention to social justice issues by lying in front of cars in the street, jamming traffic. Some students in the movement workshop actually do lie down and imagine what it would feel like to be Mr. Perry, and other students enact the cars and impatient drivers he was delaying.

For adult tours, MHM's aim is that they be strongly human, story-driven, and conversational rather than didactic and presentational, drawing on the "experiences and expertise of the audience as well as of the interpreter."

NMAH's docents or facilitators offer one-hour Highlights Tours twice a day, taking visitors to some of the museum's "most cherished collection items as well as hidden gems, such as the gold nugget that started the California Gold Rush." Shorter exhibition- or subject-specific Spotlight Tours are also offered. These are fast-paced overviews of about fifteen minutes in duration, providing visitors with an overview of some of the most popular exhibitions, objects, and subjects.

At CMA Imaginators serve as tour guides for field trips. Each Imaginator guides a group of fifty students, chaperones, and teachers off the school bus and into the museum. They are brought to a specific zone for a ten-to-fifteen-minute interpretation. The students have time to explore that zone with the Imaginator and then rotate to the next zone.

At MSI "Immersive Tours" are led daily by facilitators or costumed characters. They are timed, ticketed, scripted experiences lasting twenty to thirty minutes, and they include areas iconic to MSI, such as:

- *The Coal Mine*—where visitors step on a hoist and take a ride to the bottom of a mineshaft. This was the museum's first interactive experience, and it has been a permanent exhibit since 1933, examining the evolution of the technology used in mining coal and offering an opportunity for visitors to experience what it's like to work in a mine.
- *Pioneer Zephyr*—visitors climb aboard and go back in time to 1934 for the record-breaking "ride" from Denver to Chicago. They explore the train's baggage, smoking, passenger, and observation compartments and view the engineer's cab with a computer interactive that allows them to "drive" the *Pioneer Zephyr*.
- *U-505 Submarine*—visitors board the actual vessel that stalked the Atlantic before it was captured on June 4, 1944. The vessel has dramatic lighting and sound effects, and visitors experience life aboard in the days leading up to her capture.

Guest Presenters

Paid or unpaid, guest presenters are not employed by the institution; they are contracted or invited to volunteer to present workshops, demonstrations, and programs featuring their area of expertise.

Examples

At NCM, visiting scientists, artisans, and performers fall under this category. The content is ideally "related to museum exhibits and activities, but likely not developed with that intention."

CMA has an ongoing relationship with a professor and scientist at Georgia State University who hosts weekly Dr. Science Wonder Shops for children and their parents. These Wonder Shops are not directly related to the museum exhibits but are offered to show that science is fun and part of our everyday lives.

SMM has special event days, such as *African Americans in Science*, during which guest presenters offer programs. They also have a monthly event—*Community Acts (Arts Coming Together with Science)*—an hour-long, volunteer, science-based variety showcase for local talent.

Object Carts

As Nina Simon says in her book *The Participatory Museum*,

> Imagine looking at an object not for its artistic or historical significance but for its ability to spark conversation. . . . Social objects are the engines of socially networked experiences, the content around which conversation happens. . . . Staff members are uniquely capable of making objects personal, active, provocative, or relational by asking visitors to engage with them in different ways.[3]

Movable or stationary, carts contain real or reproduced objects, are usually hands on, and are interpreted by a facilitator, demonstrator, staff, or volunteer. Carts tend to be located in well-transited spaces and focus on elements of an institution's collections. Sometimes they are directly connected to an exhibit. Objects are selected for their uniqueness, attraction quality, or mystery. Staff using the cart is able to engage visitors in inquiry-based interactions, to share facts, and to tell stories about the objects. They make connections between what is on the cart and the artifacts and stories told in the exhibit.

Examples

At MHC they offer History à la Cart, touchable objects from the museum's teaching collections used by interpreters to engage visitors in exhibit content and themes and to offer them a tactile connection with the objects in the exhibit.

At CMA, an Imaginator facilitates daily interactions with a science cart called an Exploration Station, allowing young visitors to learn about their five senses and their heart rate.

NMAH thinks of history education as a three-legged stool: object centered, people oriented, and conversation based. Objects are at the center of everything they do, helping the museum to make American history real, providing ways to access both individual and family stories, and encouraging visitors to see their own stories as an important part of a larger American story. Their touch carts offer small groups of visitors an opportunity to engage with objects from the teaching collection and converse with the presenter and each other. Several small group carts are on the floor daily, staffed by docents or facilitators. NMAH also has destination carts, a "major visual draw to visitors." These carts often use multiple staff and attractors such as music, theatre, and costumed mannequins.

Figure 2.5   Cart, Minnesota History Center

Facilitated Programs

Presented by staff trained in exhibit subject matter, facilitated programs are interactive and of varied duration.

Examples

Facilitated experiences are offered for audiences of all ages in the form of opportunities to conduct experiments, touch animals, and create art.

SMM uses facilitated programs mostly with preschoolers. *Sound All Around* encourages playing with instruments while exploring the science of sound, and *Goldie's Bears* is a "choose your own adventure" program focused on the eight species of bears.

Demonstrations/Presentations

These are live presentations of information by a trained presenter.

Commonly used to describe science shows, these words also apply to art and humanities programs. As will be seen from the examples below, demonstrations and presentations encompass a variety of subjects and techniques.

Figure 2.6   Timbuktu Drums, Atlanta Children's Museum

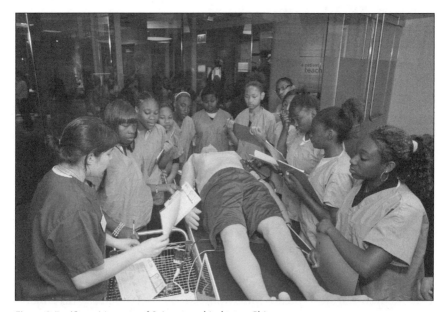

Figure 2.7   iStan, Museum of Science and Industry, Chicago

Figure 2.8   Earth Revealed, Museum of Science and Industry, Chicago

Examples

At SMV, demonstrations are presented by a single science educator as well as by museum volunteers. They are "non-story/non-character based and intended to provide entertaining examples of cause and effect as well as the scientific process within a variety of science topics." They are scripted and require only one presenter, who uses props and various kinds of scientific equipment at a cart that rolls to different locations. One of the most popular is the cow eye dissection.

At SMM demonstrations are offered daily. They are scripted, one-person shows, often involving PowerPoint images and covering current science topics, for example, *Treating Tumors with Gold.*[4] SMM's demonstrations show how something works, examine natural phenomena, or teach a skill or process. During a demonstration examining acceleration and air resistance by using spaces in creative ways, SMM drops items from a ledge fifty feet above the audience in *Skyledge Free Fall.* The museum believes in demonstrations as a means of attracting adult audiences, as proved by *Fermentation: The History and Chemistry of Beer.*

NCM believes that an important part of the visitor experience at their former site as the Capital Children's Museum was attending a chemistry show in the Chemical Science Center. The Chemical Science Center exhibit was built around the use of live interpretation and was designed with three distinct areas:

- a small exhibit space with an introduction to chemistry through text panels, video and computer displays, with a few hands-on elements
- a large demonstration theatre where specially trained demonstrators provided interactive presentations on different aspects of chemical science
- a chemistry lab where visitors could be guided by trained staff in performing their own chemistry experiments.

The success of the Chemical Science Center and its live interpretation led to the institution's decision to make greater use of live interpretation, especially interactive interpretation, in its new facility.

In 2012, MHM opened an exhibition called *Underneath It All* about the history of women's underwear and the ways in which women's fashion reflects women's roles through time. *Getting Dressed: Inside Out in the Corset Age* was developed to show audiences how women put on and took off historic underclothes and how the different pieces fit together to create historic silhouettes. This program is performed in the Grand Hall, which can accommodate as many as 150 people. The presenter changes clothes three times, donning and removing complete outfits from 1790, 1803, and 1860.

Character Appearances

Museums sometimes use costumed characters representing famous figures from art, history, and science, composite or fictional, and storybook characters. These roaming characters may carry a prop representative of their time period or profession and speak in an accent or style of their own. They interact informally with visitors, sharing information and stories and answering questions.[5]

Examples

MHC's History Players are costumed actor/interpreters who portray real characters from Minnesota History, offering short, improvisational performances in exhibit performing areas and interacting informally with visitors in between performances. These characters are selected and developed to illustrate specific exhibit themes.

During the exhibit *Amazing Castles* at CMA, Imaginators became the village merchants and visitors dressed up as townspeople helping to prepare for the king's banquet.

Figure 2.9   Getting Dressed, Missouri History Museum

During the Children's Museum of Indianapolis's Barbie exhibit, actors
were given the assignment of creating designer characters and costumes

Figure 2.10   Pirate, Science Museum of Minnesota

with a career and personal history unique to each actor/designer. The designer pictured on the next page is Zashh (Zashh stresses that the second *H* is silent). His personal history began at the age of six, when he created his own outfit from leftover fabric he found in the attic, and he describes himself as the greatest fashion designer this side of the White River. (For those of you not familiar with Indianapolis, that's an area of a very modest number of blocks). Before appearing in a scripted program in the exhibit's design studio, Zashh roams the gallery introducing himself and inviting visitors to attend the program. Three other fashion designers also appeared in the exhibit. Some of them commented (always favorably) on clothes worn by visitors; others showed off their designs.

Figure 2.11 *Zashh! Barbie Exhibit,* Children's Museum of Indianapolis

Storytelling

Storytelling can take various forms. Professional storytellers have a repertory of stories that they can organize thematically and to meet the requirements of the venue. Some storytellers use simple props or pictures.

In libraries and museums, storytelling is sometimes literally the reading of a children's story.

Examples

At MHM, storytellers read children's books around different themes—for instance, airplane stories were read in the Lindbergh gallery near a model of Lindbergh's cockpit from his historic trans-Atlantic flight. These programs are geared toward the youngest visitors and also incorporate an easy make-and-take craft activity that matches the storytelling theme.

At CMA, daily storytelling takes place in the afternoons. The stories relate to the themes of the touring exhibit, are created on a storyboard, and are accompanied by music. Story time is always interactive and relies on audience participation.

Occasionally at the SMV, storytelling is used to illustrate the history of humanity's attempts to explain scientific phenomena. By sharing the Cherokee tale of a wily dog that raided a barrel of cornmeal, actors relate

Figure 2.12 *Don't Call Me Monkey*, Science Museum of Minnesota

the Native American story of *How the Milky Way Came to Be*. When the dog was chased away, he leapt into the sky with a mouthful of cornmeal. Some of it spilled as it sailed through the sky, creating the Milky Way.

Creative Dramatics
Examples

Defined by the American Alliance for Theatre and Education as "an informal, improvisational, non-exhibitional, process-centered form of drama in which participants are guided by a leader to imagine, enact, and reflect upon human experiences through role-play, improvisation, pantomime, movement, and sound," the term is most often used to describe a form of play that involves what children do naturally—adopt roles and act them out, sometimes in the context of a story.

At SMV, it "includes activities that incorporate elements of live theater such as role-playing, creative movement, props and vocal expression; facilitated by a single actor with the intent of teaching cause and effect as well as the scientific process within a variety of science topics. These activities can also be story-based." During one of them, students enact the annual

Figure 2.13   Planets rotating around the Sun, Atlanta Children's Museum

flooding of the Nile River, using arm motions and blue streamers to depict calm water and brown ones to represent muddy, fast-moving floodwaters.

Living History

I have included this category because of its importance to the field of interpretation. It is a genre all its own and has been extensively studied. It is also typically practiced in facilities designed and set up precisely for this type of live interpretation, and extensive resources exist for those wishing to access in-depth information.

Museum Theatre

> *Theatre, and theatre alone of human activities provides an opportunity of experiencing imaginative truth as present truth.*
>
> —DAVID COLE[6]

While the use of theatre and theatrical techniques in museums is my specialty, I have spent an equal proportion of my career in museums to demonstrations and informal, unscripted audience interactions. No doubt my

Figure 2.14   Anne Frank Exhibit, *Power of Children*, Children's Museum of Indianapolis

background in theatre contributes to my admiration of actors, but experience has also taught me that they are outstanding presenters of information. (I will go into more detail about my reasons in the section devoted to how and whom to hire.)

At different times over the years I've heard that museum theatre is basically any activity that combines a building—a zoo, a museum—with any one of the elements that might make up a play:

- an actor portraying a character
- a costumed interpreter
- a storyteller
- technical or special effects
- a stage

Put any two together and presto! You have museum theatre.

I'll be using the term *museum theatre* to mean a performance by a (preferably professional) actor portraying a character other than himself or herself and containing a story or dramatic narrative.

Under the heading of museum theatre fall several theatrical techniques, such as puppetry and music, both widely used in museums, as well as some not as frequently seen, such as mime and dance.

Let's start with how museum theatre differs from traditional theatre.

- *Purpose:* Just as every individual theatre has a reason for existing and being located in the chosen community, each institution that chooses to use museum theatre also has its reasons for wanting to do so.
- *Education:* Museum theatre exists with the specific purpose of furthering the educational mission of the institution.
- *Length:* Most productions are between twelve to fifteen minutes long.
- *Style:* Museum theatre operates like a repertory company, with actors performing in and rehearsing several shows at a time. While a repertory company may perform one to two full-length shows a week, museum theatre actors typically perform four to five short presentations in a day.
- *Monologues:* Not the most common format in theatres; in museums the majority of shows actors perform are monologues.
- *Other duties:* Actors may also perform demonstrations and other kinds of presentations. In some institutions they provide vocal and presentation training to volunteer and staff presenters.

- *Research:* Research into the content and time period of a play is as common for actors in traditional theatres as it is for museum theatre actors. The difference for the latter is that research is required, and it goes beyond the content of the piece into the exhibit being interpreted and sometimes beyond that into the museum's mission.
- *Contact with the audience:* Most of the time actors are not in close contact with their audiences; they perform with the fourth wall in place. Museum theatre actors need to become accustomed to interacting with audiences of all ages who they are directly addressing, both during and after the performance.
- *Postshow conversations:* Considered by many museums as equally important to the performance itself, these conversations provide an opportunity for the actor to encourage the sharing of stories related to the subject matter, answer questions, follow up on details that might not be covered during the presentation, and point out objects and ideas in the exhibit.

Examples

Gard believes that museum theatre serves "to illustrate the rich humanity that surrounds and permeates the sciences." When CSTC (Carpenter Science Theatre Company) was established in 1996, it developed and performed nine to twelve short, original scripts in SMV's galleries. Local theatre companies were also booked for several short performances per year. Four years later, as a result of major renovations to the museum's facility, the Eureka Theatre, a 120-seat venue, was opened, and CSTC began performing exclusively in this traditional performance space. Scripts produced in the theatre were longer (thirty to fifty minutes) than those produced in the galleries (eight to twelve minutes), and they were performed mostly for school audiences. Gradually, CSTC performances migrated into the galleries, and as of January 2011, all 2,100 gallery theatre performances took place there.

At MHM about fifteen thousand people every year see either a museum theatre piece—a short play linked to exhibition content and designed to fit into a visit—or a destination theatre piece—a full-length traditional theatre piece that is part of the performing arts series. In 2011, MHM's piece *St. Louis I Am*, focusing on key African American individuals from St. Louis, was linked to the visit of *America I Am*, the *African American Imprint* exhibition. *St. Louis I Am* began with the story of a free woman of color, Jeanette Forchet, one of St. Louis's earliest landowners, and progressed through *Dred Scott*[7] and to civil rights activist Ivory Perry.

One of the goals of the theatre program at the NMAH is to get visitors talking about history through an interactive, personal presentation of stories of America's past that resonate in the nation's present, "ranging from well-known individuals to Americans whose stories are unknown to most of our visitors, but who were equally important in shaping the American experience."

> The dramatic experiences we offer use emotion, tension, and conflict to make visitors comfortable with an exploration of issues and topics that are less easily covered by our exhibitions. . . . Theater provides the Museum with a way to discuss with visitors the divergence of history and memory.

The first theatre program developed for the reopening of the NMAH in November 2008 was *Join the Student Sit-Ins*. The program garnered thousands of positive comments[8] from the more than 275,000 visitors who have participated in it, and it was awarded the 2009 Smithsonian Education Excellence Award, honoring the best educational program across the Institution.

> In addition, more than two thousand individual performances of original pieces have allowed visitors to meet characters such as Mary Pickersgill, who in 1814 made the Star Spangled Banner. Children's plays such as *Sing Out!* have told the story of the music of the Civil Rights Movement, and more contemplative programs such as *Letters Home* have explored serious and emotional topics, like the letters American soldiers sent home from combat over time.
> In 2010 a new theater series, *Time Trials*, allowed visitors to decide the historical legacy of controversial figures such as the colonial patriot and, later, traitor Benedict Arnold, and the radical abolitionist John Brown.

Visitors, says Wilson, were often surprised that a discussion about someone like Benedict Arnold or John Brown, whose names they may only vaguely remember from high school history, could elicit the raw emotion and strong feelings that arose in dialogue with the actors and facilitators of the programs. "That," says Wilson, "is the power of theater and authentic history combined!"

A new program, *I'm NOT a Pirate*, shatters the myths and misconceptions about pirates for summer visitors by, for example, tracing the origins of making prisoners walk the plank and addressing the more brutal forms of murder faced by prisoners.

In all *Live Science* experiences at MSI, a range of theatrical techniques is used throughout the program delivery, in the training of staff, and in how guests are expected to participate or role-play in the program. MSI's current leadership has emphasized using theatre to communicate science content, and in 2007 "members of the guest experience team partnered with the design department and the facilities department to renovate and open a 78-seat, handicap-accessible Science Theatre." In the show *Poop Happens*, guests are invited to star in a play about the digestive system. In *Taste Buddies*, guests enter the world of a vintage Candy Shoppe to learn how taste and smell combined give us a sense of flavor.

Pamela Duncan, CMA's manager of museum programming, tells us that they find that "by bringing 'life' to an exhibit through theatre, we are better able to communicate an idea, evoke an emotional response, and position ideas and objects in time and space."

So what specifically is it about a character telling a personal story in a dramatic (used here to mean *performance*, whether comic or tragic) style that makes it so special and leads to a higher rate of retention of information when it's accompanied by emotion?

- First is the basic tenet of showing, not telling. Words become actions and their consequences as experienced by the character(s).
- Second, the presentation is story driven, crafted to make us want to hear how it ends for the characters we have come to care about.

Figure 2.15   *Poop Happens*, Museum of Science and Industry, Chicago

Jones believes that a good story that illustrates one fact is better than ten facts with no story.

Figure 2.16   Maud Hart Lovelace, portrayed by History Player, Minnesota History Center

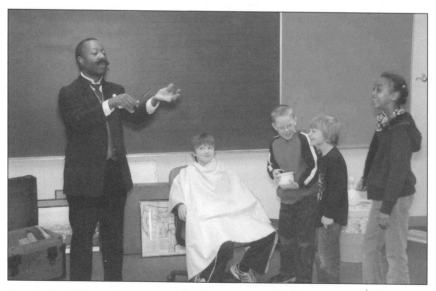

Figure 2.17   Thomas Lyles, portrayed by History Player, Minnesota History Center

- Third, the characters not only tell us their story but also present a history and a point of view.
- Fourth is conflict, a dilemma, a mystery (solved or unsolved), insurmountable obstacles, and high stakes.
- Fifth are the production standards that support the story—the aesthetics and attention to accuracy and detail in background sets, props, and costumes that make the presentation seem real.
- Sixth is linked to fifth. Who writes, directs, and presents a piece of theatre that in under fifteen minutes covers complex information in a way that places the story first and the information second, while serving as a catalyst for wanting to learn more? This question is addressed in the following chapter.

Notes

1. American Association of Museums, 1984.
2. Freeman Tilden, *Interpreting Our Heritage* (Chapel Hill: University of North Carolina Press, 1957; 2008).
3. Nina Simon, *The Participatory Museum* (Santa Cruz: Museum, 2010).
4. Developed by Dr. Lisa Regalla, the Museum of Science Boston and the NISE network.
5. Visitors are often wary of costumed characters, unsure of what is expected from them and of how to interact with the character. It isn't unusual for people to attempt to "stump the character" by asking questions clearly not within the character's knowledge base or time period. Essential to the success of a costumed character is that the actor portraying the character has a clear understanding of the purpose of the appearance and has been rehearsed in a wide range of possible responses.
6. As quoted in Ivan Karp and Steven D. Lavine, *Exhibiting Cultures* (Washington and London: Smithsonian Institution Press, 1991).
7. 1857 Supreme Court decision finding that neither Scott nor any other person of African ancestry could claim citizenship in the United States.
8. Among them: "This is exactly the kind of experiential learning we should be providing for all," "it was the highlight of my visit," "a moving and memorable experience," "this show should go on the road to American history classes in schools across the country!" "I have a lot to go back and think about."

3

In 2004, the American Association of Museums convened a task force to discuss Comprehensive Interpretive Planning (CIP). From this two-day meeting the field received a description of what CIP is:

> A written document that outlines the stories and messages the museum wants to convey through a variety of media such as exhibits, programming, and publications. It may include the institution's interpretive philosophy, educational goals, and target audiences.[1]

Few institutions have an interpretive philosophy or plan, but most have standards and practices that would allow them to develop one. Such plans need to include:

- Institutional mission statement and values and how the interpretive plan and philosophy support them.
- A description of the environments in which programs will be presented. (It is here that the collaboration between exhibit design and development, and interpretation, can be outlined.)
- The style and range of programs visitors will be able to access, and their educational objectives.[2]
- A description of your target audiences, and how interpretive programs will address different learning styles.
- Plans for including interpretation professionals already on staff, and for hiring staff as needed to write and develop, direct, and present interpretation programs. If training will be needed, outline how it will be provided and by whom.

Program Development

Institutions that have written guidelines for the development of programs typically include a:

Conceptual phase: ideas are brought forward for consideration, preliminary research is conducted, presentation and storage spaces are identified, technical needs are determined, necessary resources (material and staff) are identified, and a proposed budget is introduced.

Development phase: research continues, an interpretive style is selected, content specialists and contractors are identified, goals and messages for the program are determined, development and implementation teams are formed, and a program developer and writer are identified.

Implementation phase: materials, props, costumes, and artifacts are produced; practice sessions begin; program previews.

Public phase: program is presented to the public, revisions are made, and evaluations are carried out.

Closing phase: disposal or storage of materials, props, costumes, graphics, and archiving of written materials.

Approvals, who gives them, and at which points, also need to be considered.

At NCM the program development process is multidepartmental, with participation and/or feedback from Exhibits and Programs, External Relations, and Finance, as well as outside expert advisors and partners.

Program topics are selected based on the following criteria:

- how the subject supports elements of the mission, vision, and values
- how it aligns to a specific exhibit, area of engagement, or museum initiative
- how it ties into guiding principles for visitor experiences and commitment to providing hands-on, staff-driven programs
- how it connects to, attracts, and/or expands the communities and audiences served
- how it will be developed and implemented within the resources and time frame being proposed
- how it fits into the overall program calendar
- the suitability for the proposed program and timeliness of subject
- the presentation style
- space requirements for the program

At the onset of each exhibit's development the MHC considers budget, exhibit size, intended audience, exhibit content/themes, current staffing capacity, and other factors that influence whether interpretation is included in the exhibit and what style of interpretation is needed.[3]

At SMV the artistic director of the Carpenter Science Theatre Company is responsible for constructing an annual season (with input from staff educators), scheduling performances, constructing and overseeing the theatre budget, writing scripts, directing shows, and performing. A manager of gallery educators administers the demonstrations.

NCM has a Program Master Plan regarding the standards used for selecting and developing museum theatre productions.[4]

For MSI's Program Implementation Plan, please see Appendix D.

Expectations of the Programs and Those Who Present Them

At SMM *Science Live* productions aim to inspire further learning, to pique an interest in a subject, and to create a love for lifelong learning. To achieve this goal, SMM uses the communication skills and talents of theatre artists, who dramatize the conflict, the emotions, and the humanity of scientific endeavors.

The human storyteller, Jones tells us:

- exudes energy, which in turn energizes the exhibit
- makes eye contact, smiles, and encourages visitor participation with welcoming body language
- can read the interests and abilities of a specific audience and adjust the presentation accordingly
- can convey nuances of meaning and emotion through voice inflection, facial expression, and gesture
- brings props, costumes, and other visual and tactile elements for visitors to touch or view up close
- can engage adults and children at the same time
- is able to use inquiry, discussion, role-playing, and other interactive interpretive techniques to involve the audience
- can answer visitor questions about the story (and about the location of the restrooms)
- brings his or her own unique interpretation to the story—repeat visitors see something new each time.

She believes that appealing to diverse learning styles is of paramount importance, and she summarizes the strengths and challenges of live interpretation in this way:

Strengths:

1. It is delivered by a real, live person.
2. It conveys complex ideas by showing rather than telling.
3. It presents the story within the context of human behavior.
4. Audience research indicates that it makes a strong impression on visitors.
5. Audience research indicates that visitors learn key ideas, facts, and concepts through live storytelling.
6. It's easy to change if you didn't get it right the first time.
7. It creates the feeling of an "event," or something special and extraordinary, taking place in the exhibit.
8. It allows visitors the opportunity to voice their perspectives on the story to a captive ear and personalizes the exhibit experience for the visitor.

Challenges:

1. It is delivered by a real, live person!
2. It requires continued funding throughout the life of the exhibit.
3. It requires a crew of support staff to provide encouragement, nourishment (intellectual and physical), training, and discipline.
4. It can take up a lot of exhibit space for a stage and seating, which may not always be available to use.
5. The details of the story sometimes need to be simplified due to constraints of time and clarity.
6. The depth and accuracy of the story can be damaged in the hands of an inadequate presenter, and the overall quality of the storytelling presentation may not be consistent for all visitors.
7. It is not always available for every visitor.
8. Not all visitors are comfortable talking to strangers, especially if the stranger is wearing a hoop skirt.

SMV believes that all live interpretation programs must:

- engage, compel, and entertain museum visitors
- be performed by skilled presenters
- be valued highly by the museum staff as well as by museum guests
- have the majority of them performed on the front line of the visitor experience: the galleries

For CMA and in the case of museum theatre, programs must be participatory, personal, and immersive, engaging the visitor on an emotional level that connects them to the story.

NMAH believes that its public programs make them:

- accessible
- interactive
- relevant
- challenging
- exciting
- engaging for diverse audiences
- adaptable to seasonal visitation patterns
- a means of presenting challenging ideas and memorable experiences
- enriching to the visitor experience by stimulating conversation about history among as many people as possible

Some institutions depend on their interpreters to note frequently asked, or unusual, questions for future reference, and also use them as a means of becoming aware of what visitors want to know and can therefore plan how to modify an exhibit.

CMA presented the touring exhibit *From Here to Timbuktu: A Journey through West Africa* in 2010, offering children an opportunity to explore different and distant cultures while celebrating their similarities to our own. Visitors interacted with the objects in the exhibit, but it was during performances of *Where in the World Is Timbuktu?* that they were invited by the Imaginators on a journey of participation in social experiences such as fishing off the coast of West Africa, bartering at the Appa marketplace, and joining in a *njembe* drum circle.

Gard believes that nothing can "replace human interaction."

> Human contact with visitors is an inspiring, uplifting, ear-bending, soul-reaching, and brain-motivating method of giving museum guests a truly unforgettable experience—an impassioned experience they will take home with them, with lots of wonderful educational content mixed in.

All of these expectations constitute a very tall order. Let's take a moment to review them.

Programs and those who present them should:

- inspire further learning, peak interest in a subject, create a love for lifelong learning

- exude energy, which in turn energizes the exhibit
- encourage visitor participation with welcoming body language
- read the interests and abilities of a specific audience and adjust presentation and content accordingly
- convey nuances of meaning and emotion through voice inflection, facial expression, and gesture
- engage adults and children at the same time
- use inquiry, discussion, role-playing, and other interactive interpretive techniques to involve the audience
- answer visitor questions about the story (and about the location of the restrooms)
- bring a unique interpretation to the story—so that repeat visitors see something new each time
- appeal to diverse learning styles
- convey complex ideas by showing rather than telling
- present the story within the context of human behavior
- create the feeling of an "event," or something special and extraordinary, taking place in the exhibit
- allow visitors the opportunity to voice their perspectives on the story and personalize the exhibit experience for the visitor
- engage, compel, and entertain museum visitors
- engage the visitor on an emotional level that connects them to the story
- learn new material on a regular basis
- conduct research before and after the presentation opens so as to keep content current
- engage with visitors as providers of institutional and programmatic information
- gather audiences
- inspire visitors to want to learn more

In addition, interpreters are expected, among other duties, to:

- keep materials and props in order
- wear and maintain costumes and uniforms
- attend meetings and rehearsals
- practice on their own time
- handle equipment and materials of all types, including radios
- deal with lost children
- conduct postshow conversations

- staff special events
- memorize lines
- conduct interactive experiences
- warm up their voices and bodies before presenting a program and . . . the list goes on.

A presenter is also expected to make audiences comfortable whether or not they wish to participate, and be able to gauge the level of participation with which each person is at ease. Presenters will encounter people unwilling to speak or engage at all, those who they'll have difficulty preventing from speaking, and some who may even play "stump the presenter" by asking questions that can only be answered by breaking character.

Contrary to what our list of expectations would lead us to expect, both the people who develop our programs and those who present them are often unpaid, or on the lowest pay range of the institution.

Providing presenters with tools for dealing with the complex situations listed and with opportunities to practice using those tools, along with financial compensation commensurate with their role and skills with the public, is long overdue.

Who Presents

I have already expressed my bias regarding the advantages of hiring actors to provide interpretation in museums. My reasons are that they are expert at the narrative and storytelling skills that make it possible for audiences to construct meaning from what they see, hear, and touch, and experience has taught me that it is much easier to teach an actor to present content than it is to teach a content specialist to act, and all presentations involve acting.

At the same time, credit is due and must be given to nonactors who, either as volunteers or paid staff, do exemplary work in the field of interpretation.

Molly Kennedy Lageson, SMM's Volunteer Resource Consultant, has found that volunteers "become so invested in their interpretation roles, they often request to have input in activity development." As of 2007, the museum provides five $1,000 grants "to volunteers to develop an interpretation module or activity for themselves and other volunteers to facilitate on the museum floor."[5]

Interpretation of exhibits at NMAH has primarily been provided by a corps of docents, who staff interactive carts, give Highlights tours, and facilitate hands-on activities designed to offer visitors an engaging experience that stimulates conversation, promotes an appreciation of the nation's history, and deepens the understanding of what it means to be an American.

Facilitators staff the exhibition *Invention at Play*, and the acting company at NMAH has included professional actors whom the museum credits with having added to the popularity of programs within the museum through traveling shows and on their website. They have also performed at the White House, the Department of Justice, several National Parks Service sites, the Capitol Visitors Center, and the House of Representatives Page School.

MHM's interpretation history began with a large volunteer corps. In August 2005, Pickard was brought in as a graduate research assistant to investigate how museums used theatre programming and to propose a new model. In addition to regular performances by professionally trained staff, the museum now has a cadre of apprentice actor/interpreters in the Teens Make History Program. The Teens Make History Players participate in a work-based learning program and are trained as actors, researchers, and writers. This program, says Pickard, has been instrumental in raising the overall profile of theatre in the museum because it has been well funded by private donors. It is also an example of using performance as a means of fulfilling the museum's mission by bringing "young voices" and through them "expanded audiences" into the museum. Teens also offer "their own understanding of past choices, present circumstances, and future possibilities." They are paid, and the program emphasizes money management and professionalism. The museum also supports local professional theatre companies through the Missouri History Museum Presents Theatre Series.

Since its founding in 1933, MSI has focused on interpretation of its content. When the museum opened, its only exhibit was a coal mine staffed by retired coal miners who could bring the experience to life, this was followed by *Underwater Welding* featuring real professional underwater welders who "performed" in front of a museum audience several times a day in a small theatre area.

Beginning in 2004 CMA piloted live interpretation as a means of enhancing the visitor experience. Three members of the museum's visitor services team were given a moderate amount of training in presentation skills and then invited to engage visitors on the museum floor. It soon became apparent from the reactions of guests and the observations of museum staff that these individuals were making a big difference in the learning experience. They were able to answer questions, stimulate imagination, and encourage exploration greater than visitors were able to realize on their own. Despite these positive achievements, it also soon became clear that this team of interpretive staff were limited by their skill sets and their comfort levels in fully delivering their energies and ideas in a performance setting. To be more effective in creating the widest range of possibilities for guests, the museum determined that it needed professional performers, and it hired Duncan to create the Imaginator program.

This troupe of professional actors with backgrounds in children's theatre, creative dramatics, and education also create programs based on the exhibits and on Georgia's Performance Standards. Twelve part-time and one full-time Imaginator lead science demonstrations, education workshops, guided tours, story time, rhythm and movement activities, puppet shows, and perform in minimusicals. Each Imaginator occupies one of the museum's learning zones and conducts individual, zone-based interpretations. Twice a day, they come together to perform a minimusical specifically scripted to enforce the temporary exhibit's core educational objectives. All of CMA's plays require audience participation and volunteers coming up on stage. During a performance accompanying the exhibit *Bob the Builder*, the Imaginators performed for a group of eighteen-month-olds. None of these toddlers were developmentally ready to answer questions and follow directions on stage. Pamela Duncan, manager of Museum Programming, reports that the actors were able to eliminate all of the audience participation without missing a beat.

SMM has twelve professional part-time actors who perform both theatre and demonstration programs, puppet shows, and presentations, interacting and mingling with museum visitors in and out of character. Additional actors are hired for performances in special or touring exhibits. For example, twenty actors were hired to portray pirates in the *Real Pirates* exhibit.

Long explains that talent is just one of many qualities SMM looks for. The actors they hire must also possess an approachable demeanor and be "socially intelligent." SMM considers their ability to engage visitors essential, since interpretation in museums is a form of social mediation that leads to learning. Presenters need to know when to approach visitors and when to leave them alone. Long also prefers actors who have a strong background in improvisation.[6] MSI also hires for individuals with the ability to improvise and places an emphasis on improvisational skills in their hiring and training practices.

SMM's actors also present demonstrations such as *Cryogenics* (exploring ultracold temperatures with liquid nitrogen) and presentations such as *Treating Tumors with Gold* (experiments with gold nano shells to treat tumors). SMM has a long history of addressing challenging scientific

Figure 3.1   Pirate, Science Museum of Minnesota

and social issues. During my time with SMM plays were presented on euthanasia, gender discrimination, and human overpopulation. More recently the museum developed an exhibition on race, with accompanying programs and talking circles providing an opportunity for discussion among visitors, and it has examined several medical issues through the medium of theatre.

Some shows at SMM don't offer a resolution. This open-ended approach creates a space for visitors to examine issues by using the characters as a starting point for conversation. Examples of this style are: *Race to the Finish Line* (roommates engage in a heated debate about the concept of race), *Three Angry Scientists* (mirroring the classic film *Twelve Angry Men*, the show narrates the decision-making process determining the safety of a new drug), and *Let's Talk About It* (two sisters discuss the many different forms of treatment available to their dying mother who wasn't allowed treatment with gold nano shells, which was still in the experimental phase).

When Jones was hired by the Education Department in January 1992, she had spent the past four years working in various living history and other interpretive programs at MHS's network of historic sites. The History Center was scheduled to open in October of that year, and Jones was charged with developing a menu of live interpretive programs that would meet visitors' diverse learning styles, extend and enhance exhibit content and themes, and function as a "choice" for visitors in an environment of many other learning opportunities. The original roster of programs included History à la Cart (staffed hands-on artifact stations), Storytelling, History Players (costumed first-person characters), and History Bits (short theatrical demonstrations of historical concepts).

At opening, the MHC had a staff of fifteen part-time paid interpreters, who delivered the programs and also provided general security in the exhibits. It continues to employ a corps of these interpreters (supplemented by volunteers) who provide a range of formal and informal programs in the exhibit galleries. On occasion, outside actors are brought in as guest presenters.

The MHC used to have separate staff for the delivery of gallery and school programs (i.e., standards-based history lessons taught on-site). When Jones took over School Programs, she merged those programs with gallery programs and created a single work group that delivered live programs across multiple areas (Galley Programs, School Programs, Public Programs, and Outreach Programs).

SMV's in-house theatre company develops, produces, and performs original scripts and storytelling related to the topics, personalities, and artifacts in the museum's exhibits, and it includes a full-time artistic director and two part-time actors. Demonstrations are different in that presenters are not required to have an acting background or create characters or stories. They are expected to have high-quality presentation skills and a good level of technical knowledge regarding the subject matter of their demonstration. These demonstrations are presented by a staff of gallery educators as well as by museum volunteers. Each demonstration is scripted and requires only one presenter, who uses props and various kinds of scientific equipment at a cart that rolls to different gallery locations.

Content specialists (historians, scientists, scholars) can be highly desirable presenters, able to model "the real thing" (an actual astronaut, archeologist, physicist, explorer), tying in with a desire for authenticity and the presentation of real objects. As a cautionary example, Duncan shared that in the case of the developers of children's books, "not all children's authors and illustrators make captivating presenters," and she recommends inviting them to present a program before hiring them. This is excellent advice for all guest or nonprofessional presenters.

Museums will often address interpretation staff shortfalls with volunteer, intern, and student presenters. The important question to be raised by this choice is whether other areas of the museum (fund raising, curatorial, design) approach staffing issues this way, or if this is an example of a misguided "anyone can do it" attitude when it comes to performance or other forms of interpretation.

Who Are Our Interpreters and What Do We Call Them?

Programs, ranging from informal to formal or scripted, are presented by full-time and part-time staff and volunteers, variously called (and here, too, museum staff shows inventiveness in naming the groups):

Actor Interpreters
Actors
Ambassadors
Demonstrators
Docents
Enactors
Facilitators
Greeters
Guides
History Players
Hosts
Imaginators
Interpreters
Presenters
Roving Interpreters
Science Educators

Volunteers
Volunteer Roving Facilitators
And other combinations of these terms.

Selecting Presenters

So how do we find people with the extraordinary qualities taken from our own field's position descriptions and expectations as listed above? Are actors the only ones with these qualities? Certainly not, but if you want to start with the group most likely to provide what you need, give actors a try.

Actors are disciplined, reliable, responsive, and creative. Those who choose to work in museums embody the skills and attributes museums value—they are avid learners, have an approachable demeanor, a sense of pacing, the ability to improvise, ability to read people and establish a dialogue of learning, ability to think on their feet, and skills to recognize who wants to be approached and to what extent.

Actors are to be found in every community. As preparation for hiring them, start with a clear and concisely written job description, and then advertise. How and where you advertise depends largely on your area. Sending notices to local professional and amateur theatres and college and university theatre departments is a good start. Some cities and communities have publications devoted to the arts, and some have web pages dedicated to getting the word out about auditions. Some have specific print and live media sites and online resources for posting theatre-related jobs.

It's important to choose your wording and say what's most essential—is it a full-time or a part-time position? Does it pay? Do you offer benefits? In the ad, it's also important that you outline the next step. Do you want actors to call for an appointment? Send a resume?

Advertising for actors is one of the few occasions when you can specify age, ethnicity, and gender (which is one of many reasons why the word *actress* is such a loss and leads to the oxymoron *male actor*). Actors get very annoyed if they turn up at an audition and find that you only wanted two twenty-year-old Asian American males. If that's what you need, it's OK to say so.

Resumes are extremely useful, but they don't really tell you what you most want to know. Can this person act and present? You may be surprised by the number of people who show up at auditions who can't.

My recommendation is to schedule applicants for an audition before interviewing them. Ask them to bring their resume to the audition and explain to them what you expect them to prepare.

I recommend two pieces, for a total time of not more than five minutes. One piece should be entirely of the applicant's choice: something that shows off their skills to the best advantage; the other should be an interactive piece that will show how they deal with an audience. They can teach you a song, ask you to help them tell a story, or perform an experiment. Over the years I've learned many useful skills from auditions—among them how to make salsa and repair a toilet.

For this interactive part to work, I audition presenters in groups of five or six. I ask them to do their chosen piece first, and then everyone participates in one another's interactive pieces. That gives me a chance to see them in action several times.

From the entire group that auditions I select the best and invite them in for an individual interview. The purpose of this is to discover how their experience and personality fit in with the institution's needs. Not every fine performer is a fine fit for the work we do.

At this point I can answer questions about schedules and pay scale, which brings us to the question of how to determine what to pay actors.

The best way is by surveying what theatres in your area are paying, from Equity (the union representing performers) theatres to the nonunion ones. This gives you an idea of what actors can command in your area. You also need to consider your institution's rates of pay. How will this position be classified, and what is it comparable to? Once you have collected a range of examples and determined where in your institution the position falls, you are on your way to determining a rate of pay—I recommend erring on the high side.

The Children's Museum of Indianapolis has a hiring and training process for its facilitators (occasionally actors will begin in this role) outlined in Appendix E.

Training/Coaching

As the *Journal of Museum Education* pointed out in its Spring 2009 issue, audiences seek to be "emotionally connected . . . not emotionally confronted." This applies to interpretation as well as to exhibits and their accompanying labels and media.

Before any training on methodology can take place, a conversation is necessary with new interpreters during which the institution's *mission, values, and goals* are discussed as they pertain to the delivery of interpretative programs.

Most interpreters will find themselves *answering questions*. It isn't enough for them to know the answers; they need to practice how to deliver those answers, and program practice sessions should include time for this exercise. Interpreters also need to be told that "I don't know" is a fine answer as long as it's followed by a means of finding out.

At the Science Museum of Minnesota I began the practice of issuing presenters with question cards. One side was blank, with room for a name and address; the other had lines with spaces for the question and for the answer. The presenter was charged with finding out the answer from the content specialist assigned by the institution to that subject (paleontology, biology, etc.) and entering it not only on the postcard but also in a folder assigned for that purpose to each program, before mailing it to the visitor who originated the question. Nowadays, some of this can be done electronically. At the Monterey Bay Aquarium interpreters carry radios and can call on a naturalist for an immediate reply.

Nina Simon[7] divides questions into personal and speculative, explaining that personal questions help visitors connect their own experience to the objects on display and, I would add, to the exhibit as a whole, while speculative questions open up the possibility of imagining how an object might have been used, what purpose it might have served in homes or gardens, and what behaviors might have been associated with it—courting, worship, battle.

As she puts it, "Unfortunately, most front-line employees are trained to conduct transactions, not to foster relationships." Simon was not referring to interpreters with this observation, but it can apply to them as well. One doesn't have to look far to find examples of programs that are delivered as transactions, rather than as a means of *fostering relationships* between the audience and the subject matter. Overcoming this is by no means simple or easy. Providing directions and techniques for addressing individual audience members, making each person feel welcomed and valued with a personal greeting, a smile, making them glad and proud that they participated—will make the difference between a transaction and a relationship. These basic techniques lay the groundwork for the educational outcomes, for participation, and for lasting memories of the experience. It is only after interpreters understand these basics that they can move on to and understand the reasons behind the rest of the training the institution offers and see the tasks expected of them as having value.

Trust isn't something we tend to think of as a tool, but in the case of presenters it's the most important tool of all.

They are the ones in the hot seat, having to assess a situation quickly and decide how best to deal with it. They are human and won't always make the best choices, but the important point is that they have choices. It is your responsibility to make it clear to them that they can:

- amend, even curtail, the presentations for audiences of different ages and cultures
- acknowledge a situation that is making it difficult to present and for the audience to enjoy the presentation (heckling, children running in and out of the performance space, a breakdown in technology)
- stop a presentation if necessary to deal with these situations.

This addresses the fundamental and to some, uncomfortable aspect of being a presenter: you are the one in charge. Audiences appreciate the fact that they are being taken care of, that their comfort is being taken into account, and they tend to be uncomfortable with a presenter who doesn't acknowledge ringing cell phones or crying children and politely and firmly address them.

There is another positive side to taking charge of unexpected, or even unpleasant, situations. If well handled, it humanizes the presenter and endears him or her to the audience.

When Richard Harris was on tour in *Camelot*, I was at a performance in which he was alone on stage, about to sing a solo, when a large cloud of feathery dust floated from the ceiling of the theatre onto his head and shoulders. He looked up, out at us, up again, made a joke about birds in the rafters, brushed himself off, and when the applause died down, he sang his song to a delighted audience who had been given a glimpse of the man behind the actor.

Memorization, Practice, and Research Time—generously planned and paid for and including access to the performance or presentation space.

I once conducted a study of the amount of time it took a team of professional actors to memorize lines and read the research material provided for them. It will come as no surprise that the outcome revealed a wide range. So I came up with a formula—somewhere between the slowest and the fastest memorizer and the slowest and the fastest reader—everyone agreed that while some would be paid for more time than they needed, some would have to put in more time than they were paid for. Since the fastest memorizers weren't necessarily the fastest readers and vice versa, this ended up being as fair an estimate as we could come up with.

On average, a page of double-spaced script requires about four hours to memorize. (This is for a monologue—a presentation by a single person. It differs for dialogue and can be reduced to less than half.) These are not continuous hours; they need to be spread out over a period of at least as many days. They do not include the time needed for "muscle memory," or practice. Depending on the complexity of the actions accompanying the script, an additional one to four hours need to be added per page in the presentation space—using props, handling equipment, learning multimedia, and more.

Some institutions offer training in the study of *body language*—our own, and assessing what others are "saying" with posture, eye contact, and inadvertent movement.

Some of us are *listeners* and some of us are *talkers*, which doesn't mean that we are only capable of one, but that one or the other will in all likelihood require remedial attention.

Meaning Making. How do we make the objects, exhibits, and people we interpret real, accessible, and meaningful? Often this is enough.

Audience Interactions. Actors are often expected to find this easy, until we remember that most actors do not interact directly with their audiences. They perform behind that invisible barrier between the stage and audience, the fourth wall.

At NCM the nature and challenges of the "interactive" aspect of interpretation is recognized as the most difficult aspect for some actors.

I make it a primary goal of audience interaction that a participant feel fulfilled and proud of having done so, never that he or she wished they hadn't participated. So while an answer may be incorrect, it is never wrong to have had the courage to offer it up, and it is up to the presenter to set the facts straight without drawing attention to the error by building on the response to arrive at the correct conclusion.

Often, facilitators and actors are asked to remain after a presentation or a performance and engage the audience in conversation or discussion. This takes skill and practice and is never as easy as good facilitators and actors make it appear, nor is it as spontaneous as it seems. These postshow conversations are almost as structured as the presentation itself. Questions have been anticipated, answers practiced, and plans made for eliciting conversation and making connections between the topic and the audience.

An example is the postshow conversations that took place at the Children's Museum of Indianapolis after performances in the Anne Frank space of the *Power of Children*. Three characters were featured in monologues: Anne; her father, Otto; and their helper, Miep; with a fourth piece including both Otto and Miep. This was the most emotional of the pieces. It addressed the moment when Otto receives the news that neither of his daughters has survived Bergen-Belsen, and Miep reveals that she rescued

Anne's diary after the Franks and their children were taken, intending to return it to Anne when she came home.

This performance was emotionally taxing for actors and audiences alike, and it is after experiences that arouse strong emotions or expose audiences to new and sometimes shocking information that postshow conversations range from being easier to impossible. It depends on the size and composition of the audience and the skill of the actors in assessing it and responding accordingly, when they are also dealing with a return to the present from whatever place the performance has taken them.

During practice sessions leading up to the opening of this piece, we focused on three ways of beginning the postshow conversation.

1. *Telling the rest of the story.* Museum theatre pieces are short, and this was no exception; it ran under fifteen minutes. Otto and Miep had a lot of untold or unfinished stories to choose from. Many people wanted to know how Anne and her sister, Margo, died.[8] Some wondered how Otto had survived the war and what had happened to Miep and to other helpers after the Franks' arrest.

2. *Talking about a set or prop.* The Annex had been reproduced, and it included the radio that was so vital in keeping the people in hiding informed of the Allies' progress. Most children had seen nothing like it, and it provided an opening for talking about how it must have felt not to be free to go to school or play with friends.

3. *Sharing a personal story.* All of the performers in the Anne Frank exhibit had a story to share about a moment when the importance of what they were doing had struck them most personally. For some, it involved reading Anne's diary for the first time and comparing her life to theirs, and how easy it had been until that moment not to think of what was going on in the world beyond their own immediate concerns. For others, it involved questioning of what some of those events might be and how we can influence them, in big and small ways.

Training. SMV's commitment to live interpretation is reflected in a mandate from senior staff to improve the presentation skills of gallery educators and volunteers who deliver demonstrations. Action to realize this mandate began in January 2001 with the appointment of a supervising gallery educator and a process of observation and written evaluation of all demonstration presenters. In addition, CSTC has provided training in the use and interpretation of body language, the definition and use of vocal dynamics, and the art of public presentation.

Figure 3.2   Charles and Mrs. Darwin, Carpenter Science Theatre Company, Science Museum of Virginia

At MSI a series of training is offered to all facilitators on an ongoing basis. Managers and senior coordinators are expected to complete biweekly coaching logs, review the team members' live science experiences, and provide feedback. The director of Guest Experiences reviews feedback in the coaching log format on a monthly basis for all team members. Additional rubrics specific to each program are in the process of being created and implemented to ensure program quality is maintained. Staff is trained within a given program to tailor content to guests. Each live science experience has a certification program, with different certification criteria specific to the program. All facilitators attend a Great Guest Experience training and Improv 101 (improvisational strategies and techniques). Facilitators are trained in cognitive learning strategies and are expected to tailor content that builds on what guests already know, or alter content based on group size or age range.

At CMA Imaginators are trained in early childhood development.

At MHM, interpretive staff receives training in educational techniques, group management, historical content and research, museum studies, script development and writing, public speaking, and interpretation. Apprentice actor interpreters also receive ongoing acting training, including character development, movement, improvisation, and speech production techniques.

At the MHC, in order to perform the four essential functions of working in a zone (to provide interpretive programming; to facilitate the exhibit school program; to perceive and respond to visitors' needs and questions; and to monitor the use of the exhibit), interpreters are trained to embrace a "Zen-like philosophy": exert self-discipline ("engage with visitors even when you don't feel like it"); frequently rely on intuition (read the visitor and know when he/she would rather be left alone); and accept the paradoxes inherent to working in an ever-changing environment (the dynamic of the exhibit is constantly changing based on the composition of the audience—interpreters need to use the techniques that are appropriate for the given moment). MHC calls this the "Zen of Zone." All interpreters are trained to deliver the core exhibit-based programs. Based on the individual interpreter's skills, additional programs are added to their repertoire. As an interpreter's repertoire increases, so does the rate of pay and the number of hours worked, helping MHC to keep talented staff employed for a longer time.

In recent years the difference between asking visitors questions and engaging them in conversation has begun to be debated. I am among those who consider that what happens after a presentation in a museum is as important as the presentation itself. We offer a special opportunity at such times for our visitors to speak to the presenter and to one another about the subject matter, interactions that range from questions to personal stories.

A well-prepared presenter is just as likely to invite conversation as questions. Questions posed by the presenter can stall, rather than invite, communication, whereas conversation starters such as the examples given above can be trusted to get groups talking, making observations, and sharing insights gained.

Why Hire Live Interpreters When Electronic Means Are Available?

The debate about whether to use live or electronic interpretation is all about an institution's reasons for wanting interpretation in the first place. There is a place for both in the range of programs available to us. While this book is about live interpretation, electronic means need more than just a mention.

When asked the question above, participants began by responding why they value live over electronic interpretation. Interpreters

- are flexible, and their presentations can be more easily changed than electronic ones
- can incorporate current information into their programs at short notice
- interact with visitors and answer questions. Visitors, Finkle says, often rank interactions with both paid and volunteer staff as the most satisfying part of a visit. "Parents who bring their children to museums cite interaction with staff as valuable because they can interact with electronic means at home, yet crave opportunities for their children to develop social skills."
- build on a visitor's prior knowledge and experience and relate to their interests
- make personal and emotional connections in unpredictable ways that can't be matched by electronic means.

MHM believes that live interpreters are more responsive, adaptive, and real to the visitor. Pickard gives the example that "seeing someone portraying an enslaved person right in front of you makes it more difficult to dismiss their experience as fictional or their emotions as overwrought." She also believes that it is easier to identify with a living person and to objectify someone on a screen. "Humans also don't break when our buttons get pushed too much or magically increase or decrease in volume."

Wilson says that NMAH could engage with more people and be more frugal with its resources by concentrating on electronic means to speak to and with visitors, but they believe that an important part of visiting their museum is the community built by a once-in-a-lifetime visit to the place where the country keeps its treasured objects from the past. "As much as any information transferred to visitors, the experience of coming together in a museum, and especially in the national museum," Wilson said, "is crucially important in itself." Part of that experience is people engaging with one another as humans, as citizens, and as "seekers of knowledge," as the first secretary of the Smithsonian, Joseph Henry, stated. That live interaction is an irreplaceable tool in achieving the educational mission and in inspiring an active, forward-looking citizenry. The institution also wants to increase the ways in which it uses electronic means to engage people in conversation about history, and it hopes to find ways that are comparable in importance to visiting the museum in person.

Media, Jones says, are expensive to develop and have a limited shelf life. Technology changes rapidly, and it can be difficult to keep electronic interpretation looking current and fresh. It also requires ongoing maintenance. Ironically, it has been the education and program area at the MHC that has led the drive to integrate mobile technology into exhibit design. At the same time, "I am not at all interested," Jones said, "in using mobile technology to introduce more content into the exhibit."

What MHC is developing is a new model for mobile technology in museums, using school groups as the target audience and piloting the program in the upcoming *Then Now Wow* exhibit, which opened in the fall of 2012. The mobile experience and the exhibit were developed together, and the same education staff that worked on the mobile experience also worked on the exhibit's interactives, overall content, and live interpretation.

The project is called *Play the Past* and is targeted at students in grades four through eight. Like many museums, MHC's primary point of contact with students is through school field trips, and *Play the Past* uses mobile and web technologies to capitalize on the natural behaviors and learning styles of twenty-first-century learners. The project's goal is to demonstrate how museums can use technology with large numbers of students to create self-directed, personalized, responsive field trip experiences that deepen student engagement with museum content.

MHC believes that the project responds to four primary needs: 1) today's students are "digital natives"—they think and learn in ways different enough to challenge traditional museum pedagogy; 2) to succeed in a rapidly changing world, students need to develop twenty-first-century skills, including critical-thinking and problem-solving, creativity and innovation, collaboration, and communication skills; 3) in an era of shrinking budgets and rigid testing regimes, schools are under increasing pressure to justify field trips—if museums want to remain relevant for this significant audience they must demonstrate, in entirely new ways, that the free choice learning experiences they provide have measurable value beyond the field trip itself; and 4) museums and schools need to collaborate to create communities of learning that support the development of twenty-first-century skills and inspire lifelong learning.

MHC partnered with four Minnesota schools, each with varying access to technology, and with the Games, Learning, and Society (GLS) group based at the University of Wisconsin–Madison.

At the end of this project, MHC will have demonstrated how digital technology can be integrated into a museum's core school field trip program; how a mobile application can be designed to interact with the physical museum environment to create deeper student engagement; and how digital material "harvested" by students on field trips can be integrated into classroom curricula using simple web 2.0 tools. For how Jones envisions *Play the Past* working, see Appendix F.

Scripts

The *Journal of Museum Education*,[9] referring to the design of experiences, offered some guiding principles that apply equally to the skillful writing of scripts: "Content that is challenging, real, authoritative, meaningful, encouraging of questions, and . . . well-organized."

Not all programs are scripted. Many are meant to be spontaneous, visitor-guided interactions. A script is desirable for more structured programs, which may contain interactions and participation; have a beginning, middle, and end; and have identifiable content that is expected to remain the same for each presentation. Visitor-guided, informal interactions may not need a script, but they do require planning and training of the kind covered earlier.

Content experts often develop scripts; they are clearly the most knowledgeable people on the chosen subject. It can be counterintuitive, but writers who have had to learn and understand the subject matter before attempting to explain it to others often develop the most effective scripts. These writers can more easily put themselves in the place of audiences who may be hearing the information for the first time.

At CMA they look for educational outcomes, opportunities for interactivity and participation, connections to visitors' lives, artistic integrity and excellence, and the target audience.

Long believes that all art is about communication, and that communication results in a transfer of knowledge.

Selecting a writer includes interviews during which expectations and perspectives such as these are shared.

We will focus on two types of programs: theatre pieces, or plays, and demonstrations, as a means of illustrating the difference between theatre programs and demonstrations. The main differences are who presents these programs (actors or presenters—variously called, as we've seen), who writes them (playwrights or museum staff), and content. In a demonstration, the focus is primarily on the information being conveyed; museum theatre pieces require a storyline, character(s), dialogue/monologue, and the weaving of information into all of these.

If you've seen skillfully written and presented demonstrations and theatre pieces, you know how easy all of this is made to appear. If you have written them, you know how very difficult it is and how important to the outcome is the ability, even in comedy, to avoid presenting a heavily didactic piece while maintaining its educational integrity.

For these reasons, I recommend hiring playwrights to do this work. Their craft consists precisely in knowing how to develop characters able to tell a story while conveying information without weighing the play down. And in the case of a demonstration, a playwright can bring a fresh, outside view to a subject, similar to what a member of the general public might bring.

Often, we become immersed in the topic we are developing or the exhibit we want to dramatize and interpret, sometimes to the point of having become experts ourselves. We become fascinated with the details and the number of facts we can quote and are eager to share all those with the public, forgetting that neither demonstrations nor theatre pieces are improved by sharing everything we know.

Museums are often uncomfortable with hiring playwrights, suspecting that someone who typically writes fiction might ride roughshod over the content of the piece and ignore the truths we're trying to tell—in other words, that they'll make things up. In my experience writers are scrupulous about their research and welcome being set straight on the facts—they don't like it any better than we do when a member of the audience points out a mistake.

Writers live in every community, and most of them have at one time or another tried their hand at a screenplay if not a theatre play. Some communities have writers' centers or groups that meet at libraries, colleges, and universities, and local theatre companies (professional and amateur), all great places to start looking for a writer.

As a last resort, advertise, with caution. There are a lot of actual writers out there and many who are still developing their craft, so you could be flooded with applications. If you do place an ad, be as specific as you can about what you need ("writer experienced with children's theatre," for example), and ask them initially to send resumes only, not writing samples. The resume should tell you whether the person has any experience writing professionally.

Once you've selected a few resumes, ask for writing samples, and again be as specific as you can be, especially about length. I recommend asking for two pieces of writing (totaling ten to fifteen pages). One piece should be of the writer's choice, something the writer feels shows off his or her writing skills, and the other should be one that shows whether the writer can deliver what you're going to need—a piece that required research. One of the two should contain dialogue, preferably in the form of a play.

If you're not a writer you may be concerned about your ability to judge good writing when you see it. Trust yourself. If a piece is meant to be moving, are you moved? If it's meant to be funny, are you laughing? Does the writing show the levels of sensitivity you think are important? Do the values in the piece coincide with the values at your institution?

Once you've chosen three or four samples of writing you like, bring the writers in for an interview. It may be that after the interviews you feel you've found the one perfect writer for your project. If you haven't, or if you want to take the time to hear a variety of ideas, you can ask a few writers to submit more work. I recommend that you pay for these—I call them treatments, and there is a sample of one in Appendix G. A fee of $200 to $300 is usually acceptable.

The writers will need to know what the piece is about, what content is most important to you, where the piece will be presented, the main message you want conveyed, who the audience will be, how many actors/presenters they should write for, and what length it should be.

They are then given a couple of weeks to come up with ideas, to be submitted first in writing. Applicants are then invited to pitch these ideas in person, to talk about them and give them life. You then select the one you prefer. The treatment fee is considered an advance on the total, the other applicants get to keep theirs.

Fees for a complete, fifteen-to-twenty-minute play vary between $1,500 to $5,000 depending on the playwright's experience and the complexity of the subject matter—how much research needs to be done and whether it's readily available. How many characters is the playwright writing for and how long is the piece? For a demonstration, fees vary between $500 and $2,000.

Important points to cover in the contract are deadlines and a payment schedule. It's common practice to pay half the fee on signing and half on delivery of the final version. A content specialist is assigned to the project, someone the writer can call with content questions and who can recommend books or articles on the subject.

A very important point to consider is who is going to review the drafts of the script as they come in. I strongly discourage a committee and recommend that the person in charge of programs be the first one to look at the first draft and also the one through whom all other drafts and comments are channeled.

Make every effort to shelter the writer from receiving comments from several people, especially if you aren't clear about whether or not all suggestions have to be taken and every change made or whether advice and opinions are simply being expressed.

In the case of a theatre piece, there are two ways of commissioning it: as a work for hire or as a royalty-based work. A work for hire is paid for outright and belongs to you to do with as you will. A royalty-based contract, which is what I recommend, allows the playwright to retain certain rights over the piece. It gives the writer a vested interest in the piece, since if you sell it to another museum, a percentage of that fee will be due the writer as a royalty. Works for hire are more expensive than royalty-based ones because there's no expectation of further income.

In Closing

Among institutions using a blend of exhibits and interpretation and meriting further study are living history sites, zoos, and aquariums.

Living history sites are designed with the understanding that a human presence in the exhibits is integral to the experience they offer. Many of a site's component parts can stand alone when an interpreter isn't present, but the word *living* implies a human presence, and it's taken into account during the design and development phases.

Zoos and aquariums, on the other hand, rarely take the presence of an interpreter into account when designing where and how to house and display their living collections. Typically, when audiences think of "shows" being presented in zoos or aquariums, they imagine a bird or dolphin show, with the animals as the focus. Just as there is controversy in museums about the ethics of displaying certain objects (indigenous, religious, or controversial artifacts), so there is debate among live animal institutions and in society at large about the ethics of keeping animals in captivity and of displaying them in shows.

Some zoos and aquariums have a long history of interpretation of their exhibits, including volunteer guides, paid interpreters, and actors. Except in the case of shows that include live animals, it is rare for a zoo or aquarium to provide a performance space. The Philadelphia Zoo was a pioneer in this area, as were the Minnesota Zoo and the Monterey Bay Aquarium.

More recently, in 2010, the Zoological Society of Milwaukee received a grant from Kohl's Cares that led to the creation of *Kohl's Wild Theater*, serving, as Dave McLellan, theater coordinator, and James Mills, director of education for the Zoological Society of Milwaukee explain, to convey conservation messages such as "the palm oil crisis, colony collapse disorder, and sustainable seafood" to audiences both at the zoo and in the community.

Alison Urban, an educator at San Diego Zoo Global, recommends finding creative ways to engage learners "as a means of encouraging lasting connections with nature and wildlife. We learn though emotion, movement, story and play. When combined with a contagious passion for conservation, these dramatic elements make the guest experience memorable, even with minimal resources." For example, from her place on a big screen, Roberta the Zebra,[10] a larger-than-life digital puppet, interacts with guests in real time, reacting to their comments and questions. Roberta is controlled by one of the education staff "who gives her a voice and brings her character to life."

In the study she conducted for her master's project, which focused on how theatre impacts scientific learning for family audiences, Amber Davis[11] found that:

> Many of the professionals I interviewed explained that using theatre in the context of their institution allowed visitors to connect with scientific content on a more human level, which then led to further curiosity and scientific learning. The use of storytelling . . . shifts the emphasis from scientific facts to the lives of those involved with science. . . . Using theatre educationally can foster enjoyment in science and often inspires further learning, building confidence in the audience's ability to pursue science as a hobby or career.

Rarely do interpreters—whether they're presenting a demonstration or a theatre performance—have more than a twenty-minute window in which to reach their audience. I have seen writers charged with conveying the life of a scientist and his or her accomplishments, a history of the world, or climate change in twenty minutes or less. On the face of it, it doesn't seem possible, until we remember that the programs we have been addressing here are not meant to convey all the facts but to elicit a reaction. Sometimes that reaction is simply curiosity, a desire to know everything about this person or topic that we've succeeded in making so compelling that you can't wait to learn more. Sometimes it's amazement, or indignation, or joy. As long as there is an emotion involved, there will be an impact.

The privileged position of influencing the messages an institution chooses to convey comes with a responsibility that I would summarize in a single word: *courage*. It takes courage to try different approaches to education, and most of all, to tackle the issues of the day without apology. It's true that people come to us for amusement, relaxation, and fun. The art lies in making learning and exposure to ideas so compelling and relevant that our missions become more than words.

Notes

1. Quoted from the *Journal of Museum Education* 33 (Fall 2008).

2. For an example of interpretation goals and objectives, see Appendix A.

3. Program descriptions containing goals and objectives for MHC's core program types (History á la Cart, History Players, and Museum Theatre) can be found in Appendix B.

4. See Appendix C.

5. See Appendix H for more details.

6. This is the ability to go off script without the audience noticing, or to take story or character suggestions from the audience and create a "skit" or a scene. In other words, actors need to think and respond rapidly to changing situations.

7. Op. cit.

8. Margo and Anne Frank died of typhus contracted at Bergen-Belsen concentration camp.

9. "Museums and Schools," *Journal of Museum Education* 34, no. 1 (Spring 2009).

10. Developed by Living Pictures for San Diego Zoo Education.

11. Amber Davis, *Assessing Impact: Igniting the Spark for Science Learning with Museum Theatre*, master's project, Berkeley, CA: John F. Kennedy University, 2013.

Appendix A

Minnesota History Center's (MHC) Overall Goals for Interpretive Programs

- To support the museum's exhibits with daily educational programming that enlivens static galleries, appeals to diverse learning abilities, and creates opportunities for dialogue about the past and its impact on the present.
- To raise the public profile of the history center as both a recreational and educational destination.
- To establish the museum as an integral and vital community resource through programmatic collaborations and partnerships that promote civic engagement and build ongoing relationships with varied groups and organizations.
- To promote membership in the society; to engender loyalty and satisfaction in society members with provocative and engaging, high-quality programs.
- To promote access to the museum, the society, and Minnesota's history through free or low-cost programs.
- To support best practices in history education through teacher and student training, history curriculum, and a variety of museum-based programs that help educators meet Minnesota's graduation standards.
- To make the materials, skills, and services of the museum available through outreach programs to a statewide audience.
- To provide opportunities for people to find personal meaning from the things of the past and to see themselves as part of history.

Appendix B

Goals and desired characteristics for MHC's History á la Cart
Goals

- To facilitate an exchange between visitors and staff.
- To extend or enhance the content of an exhibit.
- To accommodate diverse learning styles.

Objectives

- The visitor will touch and/or manipulate or apply objects. *(How do these objects feel to me? How do I use them?)*
- The visitor will compare or contrast objects. *(How do these objects look/feel different? the same? How are these objects different/the same in the way they are manipulated?)*
- The visitor will put objects into historical context. *(Who used these objects? Why were they used? What do they tell me about the people who used them and the time in which they lived?)*

Description
History á la Cart is defined by these attributes:

1. It is an ongoing program staffed by museum interpreters and volunteers. The activity occurs at a cart or specially designed area near the exhibit section connecting to the activity's content.
2. It has no scheduled beginning or end. During the course of a day, different cart activities are set up throughout the exhibits and staffed for varying lengths of time. At least one cart activity should be open in each gallery at all times.

3. It includes objects (artifacts that are not museum quality, reproductions, photographs, raw materials, textiles, etc.) that visitors are encouraged to touch, hold, manipulate, and otherwise examine. These objects are connected to an exhibit theme represented near the cart itself. The objects both draw visitors over to the cart and provide them with a concrete reference point upon which they may base a dialogue with the staff person. They also provide an opportunity for visitors to use the tactile sense and to experience the exhibit through a different medium.

4. Visitors direct the activity. They may or may not stop at the activity as they pass through the exhibit. If they do stop, they determine to what extent and how long they will participate. Interpreters and volunteers use subtle techniques (such as making eye contact, smiling, asking a simple question) to lure visitors over to the cart, and they try to bring out a few predetermined key points of interpretation during their conversation with the visitor. Ultimately, however, it is the visitor who directs the length and nature of the interaction.

5. Interpreters and volunteers are provided with learning goals and objectives and background content reading for each cart activity, but they are not provided with a script or a prescribed beginning and end for the activity. They are instructed to keep the activity "fluid" and not to repeat a canned "spiel" over and over again. Each group of visitors responds differently to the interaction with the interpreter, and visitors may join or leave at any point during the interpretation. Consequently, interpreters need to be flexible in the way they present information connected to the cart activity.

6. History á la Cart provides the opportunity for dialogue that extends or enhances an exhibit's content. Through a cart activity, elements represented in an exhibit but not fully explored therein can be further discussed or interpreted in an informal environment.

Evaluation criteria for staff delivery of History á la Cart Program

- Greets visitors in immediate area
- Cart Presentation: items are chosen and displayed with care
- Demonstrates mastery of content and background information
- Meets stated goals and objectives of the program
- Connects the items in the cart to the exhibit
- Relates to visitor's experience or personality
- Gives the visitor something to hold/touch/do

Approachability

- Exhibits excellent nonverbal communication throughout the program
- Makes eye contact
- Uses facial expressions (Smiling is often contagious, and visitors will react favorably and learn more.)
- Uses gestures
- Good posture and body orientation
- Proximity to visitor is pleasant
- Positive paralinguistics (tone, pitch, rhythm, timbre, loudness, inflection)

Inquiry

- Uses appropriate questions for the audience (Develops leading questions that will keep the inquiry method lively and headed in the direction of the intended objectives and conclusions)
- Establishes good rapport with visitors
- Doesn't dominate the conversation
- Listens to visitors' responses attentively
- Maintains attention and interest of visitors
- Knows when to give the visitors an "out"
- Is attentive to the special needs of visitors (physical and cognitive disabilities, special interests, etc.)

Appendix C

Excerpts from National Children's Museum (NCM) Master Plan for Museum Theatre (2011)

The NCM Theatre Company will interpret NCM exhibitions and themes through theatre and drama. Productions presented in the theatre represent the primary programming vehicle for the theatre program. Topics and themes of the theatre productions will primarily relate to NCM's exhibits and core content areas (health and well-being, civic engagement, the environment, the arts, global neighborhood, and play), but productions may also be developed to complement special events, holidays, program themes, and traveling exhibits. When possible, the NCM Theatre Company will develop partnerships with individuals and organizations locally, nationally, and internationally to develop a diverse, engaging, and exciting variety of scripts, productions, and presentation styles.

- The NCM Theatre Company will determine which topics can be most appropriately presented through the theatre medium. Theatre will be used to explain complex concepts, personalize information through narrative and story, provide context for facts and ideas, and create connections between visitors and characters that lead to deeper understanding and increased memory of concepts. The theatre programs should be enjoyable for visitors and provide a rest during the active museum visit. Whenever appropriate, scripts will allow for active and meaningful audience participation.
- Approximately four new productions will be developed each year (fall, winter holidays, spring, and summer). Half of all

productions will interpret permanent and traveling exhibits. While all productions must be appropriate for a general family audience, approximately 30 percent of all productions will be developed specifically for early learners, defined as ages five and under. In addition, up to 20 percent of productions will be "just for fun" and may not relate directly to an exhibit topic.

- Theatre productions that relate to the exhibits will reinforce the exhibits' main messages. Priority will be given to production topics that include ideas and concepts that are 1) missing from the exhibit, 2) misunderstood by visitors to the exhibit, or 3) are of particular interest to visitors. Periodic evaluation with visitors will determine which production topics meet these conditions.

Script Development

- Scripts might be purchased or new scripts commissioned by NCM or developed in-house by one or more members of the theatre company. Scripts must meet a high standard of quality. The material must be appropriate for the intended audience (which will vary from show to show), clearly communicate the desired message, and engage the audience. Content specialists from the targeted exhibit area will assist in the development of scripts, providing information, resources, and feedback throughout the development process and reviewing drafts at key points. When needed, outside content experts or advisors will be consulted. Each production shall require no more than three performers to present it, and each production should run between twenty and thirty minutes.

Special Performances

- Guest performers may also be called upon for special events, marketing purposes, or in instances where expertise is required beyond the capabilities of the theatre company. Guest artists must meet high quality standards in regard to performance and production values. The content of a production performed by a guest artist must be appropriate for the NCM audience and must complement NCM's mission and core areas of engagement. The quality of guest performers will be authenticated by NCM prior to booking through direct observation, videotape, or reliable referrals and references.

Performances in Exhibit Areas

- Similar selection criteria will apply when developing theatre programs for presentation within the exhibits. These productions will exclusively relate to the ideas in the exhibit in which it will be performed, and it will run no longer than fifteen minutes. Examples of these performances include storytelling of animal stories in The Environment or an interactive puppet show of a folktale in Our World using an exhibit component as the stage.

Appendix D

Museum of Science and Industry's (MSI) Program Implementation Plan

Programs must:

- be grounded in science
- be fun, accessible, participatory, and inclusive
- have clear goals and learning objectives
- use constructivism or inquiry-based approaches in teaching science
- consider applying theatrical elements

Staff is required to compile a concept memo and an implementation plan for each project. The concept memo highlights the program's educational goals, content, format, and targeted teams to deliver the program. Then it moves into the development and research phase. The plan guides education program developers through the necessary collaboration points, including reviews by the director of Guest Experiences and director of Science and Integrated Strategies. Partnering with the Exhibits and Collections Division is a phase in the implementation plan. Through this process, the theatrical techniques are determined, the training strategies are developed, and the review processes are defined.

Appendix E

Children's Museum of Indianapolis—Hiring and Training Process for Facilitators
Hiring

- Positions are posted in the following locations: TCM website, IndianaAuditions.com, Indiana Youth Institute (IYI.org), Indianapolis Art's Council e-newsletter, and Indiana colleges and universities career sites.
- The Interpretation Operations Coordinator (IOC) receives applications that meet minimum qualifications from the Human Resources administrator.
- IOC prescreens applicants through a phone interview for availability, experience, and communication skills and invites those who are qualified to a group interview.
- Hiring managers and the IOC lead group interviews. Through storytelling, rapid interview questions, and extemporaneous presentations, final candidates are selected to continue in the process. Candidates who demonstrate theatrical, improvisational, and team-building skills balanced with a willingness to participate are scheduled for a second interview.
- IOC schedules the second interview and sends the candidates the Story in a Can program description, script, and tips for success.
- Hiring managers and the IOC attend the second interview in Playscape, where candidates present the prepared story to visitors. Candidates who demonstrate such skills as an ability to memorize educational content, engage families, improvise with props, connect

to visitors of all ages, entertain, adjust content to fit audience, and converse in a casual manner are elevated to the next level of consideration.
- Candidate's references are checked by either the hiring manager or the IOC.
- Candidate is offered a position.

Training:

- **Day One**—Human Resources until 2:30
    o Review of interpretation expectations, schedules, staff introductions
- **Day Two**
    o Operation training of Carousel; quality standards (safety, courtesy, show, efficiency) training
- **Day Three**
    o Operations of Scienceworks, customer service standards (greet, be knowledgeable, be positive, be efficient, service excellence) put into practice
- **Day Four**
    o Operations of Playscape, training of gathering techniques, casual conversations before/during/after programming, instruction on "gather—hold—communicate"
- **Day Five**
    o Training of informal interpretation/hosting a gallery
- **Day Six**
    o Presentation skills "tested" with more formal programming. Voice control, pacing, energy, and gathering techniques
- **Day Seven**
    o Presentation skills "tested" with informal programming, keeping a group, family involvement, less-structured setting
- **Day Eight**
    o Safety—rockwall instruction

- **Continued Training/Testing** in programs in which we use a rubric to look for the following in programs:
    o Engagement strategy, rapport with visitors, enthusiasm, driving the conversation, pacing of conversation, knowledge and explanation of content, and nurturing visitor's curiosity

Appendix F

The Minnesota Historical Society's (MHS) Play the Past
Extensive user testing of mobile and web technologies by cocreating a new twenty-first-century field trip experience with students, teachers, and parent chaperones through rapid prototyping.

- Designing an in-gallery mobile application for MHC's *Then Now Wow* exhibit that engages students in the physical exhibit environment and enables them to 1) use critical-thinking and problem-solving skills; and 2) "harvest" digital assets from the society's collections and record their personal exhibit experiences.
- Creating a "digital backpack," a secure website that stores the items students collected on the field trip and can be "opened up" by teachers, students, and parents for further exploration and deeper learning, using simple web 2.0 tools, thus bridging the classroom and museum learning environments.
- Developing a Play the Past classroom toolkit, curricular activities that help educators use the items in the "digital backpack" to support students' understanding of history and development of twenty-first-century skills.
- Implementing the Play the Past field trip at the Minnesota History Center and developing procedures for sustaining its daily operations (e.g., distribution and maintenance of handheld devices, website security, etc.).
- Positioning MHC, and museums in general, as a community resource for the development of twenty-first-century skills.

How It'll Work—MHC

- Upon arrival at the museum, students, teachers, and chaperones receive handheld devices preinstalled with the mobile application. Once inside the exhibit gallery, students are free to explore, taking in the range of traditional exhibit experiences and first-person stories. Students use their mobile devices to investigate challenges based on the stories delivered by these traditional means. Rather than provide a one-way presentation of knowledge, the mobile application will promote interaction with the physical exhibit and focus on new areas designed to engage 21st Century Learners and promote twenty-first-century skills.

- Think and Solve: Using the mobile application, students "solve different kinds of non-familiar problems in both conventional and innovative ways" (a Minnesota school standard). The device may encourage them to analyze physical objects in a space to make connections not readily apparent. For example, in a life-sized sod house environment, students may be prompted to count the shoes to figure out how many people lived in the 12′ by 14′ structure and then compare it to their own home. In an iron mine environment, they might be asked to evaluate real miners' stories and decide which job they would choose using risk versus reward comparisons, such as how great a risk of injury or death would they take to earn more money for their families. The mobile device allows for personalized exploration of real-life problems, prompting students to critically analyze "evidence, arguments, and alternative points of view" (also a Minnesota school standard) and then explore a solution and its consequences.

- Record and Collect: To extend this analysis into the classroom, a major function of the mobile application is to allow students to collect materials from the *Then Now Wow* exhibit. As students complete different exhibit investigations, they collect the stories, photographs, and other media directly related to specific exhibit components. They also collect links to related "digital artifacts" that interest them, such as photographs, document scans, and images of three-dimensional collections already available on MHC's website.

- MHC plans to incorporate the principles of game mechanics into the application's design, including virtual items such as keys, tokens, or historical objects in the compilation of elements students collect. For instance, if students obtain a certain number of "animal furs" in the fur trade section of the exhibit they may get a reward, such as a Voyageur Badge, or be able to "level up" to a new challenge. Students can also trade, share, and destroy virtual items by negotiating with their peers. These game mechanics are familiar motivators to today's students that also promote social interaction and collaboration. Finally, the mobile application allows students to reflect on their thoughts and experiences in the exhibit by taking photos and recording audio or video with their mobile devices, building on behaviors students already demonstrate when they take photos in exhibits with their own devices. The mobile device might potentially encourage this behavior in response to significant questions for investigation and analysis.

- To facilitate the functions of Think and Solve and Record and Collect, the in-gallery mobile application will use design elements aligned with 21st Century Learner preferences and learning styles.
- Design elements include:

1) Story: The mobile application will capitalize on MHC's strength in storytelling through traditional exhibit experiences by enabling students to use their mobile devices to investigate and reflect on the stories of real Minnesotans. The presentation of these stories in traditional exhibit methods—artifacts, interactives, text, live interpretation, and more—will be facilitated by the mobile application's contribution of rich media, clues for further investigation, and the ability to collect related material to take back to the classroom.

2) Personalization: The mobile application will further promote free-choice learning beyond what is already established in existing exhibits by allowing students to choose and interact with components of the exhibit they find the most interesting and compelling. MHC's student focus groups revealed a wide range in how students approached exploring and interacting with exhibits and in what they found interesting and wanted to collect.

3) Game Mechanics: To engage students with familiar modes of motivation, game mechanics (such as leveling up and rewards) will be used to encourage them to explore the exhibit, to give them puzzles to solve, and to collaborate with other students, teachers, and parent chaperones. Interaction with the physical exhibit: To ensure that the mobile activity doesn't become a virtual experience that distracts from the exhibit, the mobile application will constantly

require students to interact with the physical space. To facilitate this interaction, MHS is exploring location-based technology such as QR (Quick Response) codes, WiFi triangulation, near field communication (NFC), and object recognition technology used in applications such as Google Goggles.

The inventory of digital artifacts, virtual items, and media collected by students will be uploaded to a "digital backpack" and be available for students and teachers to use in the classroom. Through further analysis of the items in the backpack, students can expand upon the critical-thinking and problem-solving activities they started in the exhibit. Teachers can also use the backpack items to facilitate projects in which students create something that shares what they have learned, experienced, and enjoyed on their field trip. Working with teachers, MHC will design the delivery of these digital assets to ensure security, accessibility, and usability.

Appendix G

"Apollo's Eve" Script Treatment, by George E. Buss Jr., developed during a Theatre in Museums Workshop

Audience: Middle and high school students
Adult visitors

Length: Fifteen- to twenty-minute performance
Five- to ten-minute post-show conversation

Space: Big Science Theatre
Small Theatre house fitting 150 audience members with lighting and sound capabilities
Moderate noise level from exhibits in area
Stage space of 6′ x 20′ at audience level

Setting: Bedroom/dorm inside the NASA compound with a sterile, air force feel. A bed, a desk, and space and air force memorabilia.

Actors: Two (one male, one female)

Goals: To compare methods of exploration in space to exploration on earth by using the Lewis and Clark expedition as an example. To examine how explorers confront their fears of exploration. To illustrate the specific challenges faced by both Lewis and Clark as well as astronauts in space.

Content: Two astronauts preparing for a launch to the moon discover that they share fears and concerns regarding their imminent mission.

Story Line: Jason is sitting at his desk writing a letter to his wife when Louisa enters with a newspaper in her hand. The newspaper covers both the bicentennial of the Lewis and Clark expedition as well as the next day's launch to the moon, for which they both are scheduled. Jason lists some of the goals of the Midwest exploration, including mapping, rock sampling, and searching for life signs. Louisa looks over a space map on the wall and comments on the similarities to their own mission. They joke about going into space in coonskin, or walking through the woods in a space suit.

Louisa discovers Jason's teddy bear and teases him about it. He takes it in good humor, and explains that it's the closest he has to his family being with him. Louisa refers to Lewis and Clark's ability to pick up and leave their families behind in Charlotte, and how common that still is today, revealing her own divorce and the sacrifices she made for exploration.

Disturbed by the conversation, she changes the subject by returning to the paper. She discovers that Lewis was shot in the backside by a member of the expedition. They joke about the possibilities of mishaps, but it turns serious when Louisa voices her concerns regarding the tampering of material and possible launch problems, citing past *Apollo* projects. Jason reassures Louisa with information on how much further we are in technology than thirty or two hundred years ago. He gives her the teddy bear his son has given him to comfort her. Louisa heads to bed, taking the bear with her.

Jason sits down at his desk, and looks at the paper one final time. He finds a passage explaining how Lewis and Clark were gone for three years but never lost a single man. He folds the paper and returns to the letter he was writing.

Appendix H

The grants provided to volunteers at the Science Museum of Minnesota (SMM) are from the Marjorie Bolz Allen (MBA) Fund. An example of how the grant has been used is volunteer Jen Rosenbaum's exhibit *Humans and Chimps*. As described by Molly Kennedy Lageson, Rosenbaum "created an activity for the Human Body Gallery volunteers to interpret regarding the similarities and differences between humans (Homo sapiens) and our closest living relative: the chimpanzee (Pan troglodytes) utilizing books, props, and an iPad, introducing a computer as a volunteer interpretive tool for the first time" at SMM.

Kennedy Lageson adds that "as the Science Museum of Minnesota prepares for each special exhibit, volunteer involvement is considered alongside development, space, content and other considerations. There are two types of interpreters utilized in special exhibits, guest presenters and general interpreters. Guest presenters have extensive knowledge of the content already and are typically busy professionals or students. They receive minimal training and volunteer 3–4 times in the exhibit. General interpreters can include anyone who shows basic communication and customer service skills. They receive 12 hours of training and have a more structured volunteer experience."

Appendix I

Programs and plays with corresponding authors
Children's Museum of Atlanta (CMA):
"It Happens At Night!"
Written by Jerry G. White with music by Abe White

"Where in the World Is Timbuktu?"
Written by Derek Ratliff with music by Spencer Stephens

The National Children's Museum/Capital Children's Museum (NCM/CCM):
"Chemical Science Center Demonstrations"
Written by Capital Children's Museum

"Election Fever"
Written by National Children's Museum

The National Museum of American History (NMAH):
"Join the Student Sit-Ins"
Written and directed by Christopher W. Wilson

"We Shall Overcome: The 40th Anniversary of the Voting Rights March"
Written and directed by Christopher W. Wilson

The Science Museum of Minnesota (SMM):
"Cryogenics"

Written by David J. Hirschi

"Fermentation Demonstration"
Written by Michael Ritchie and Richard Rousseau

"Goldie's Bears"
Written by Patricia Choate

"Lava Live"
Written by Todd Fink and Stephanie Long

"Let's Talk About It"
Written by Richard Rousseau

"Planet Earth Decision Theatre"
Written by Patrick Hamilton and Stephanie Long

"Skyledge—Free Fall"
Written by Glenn Schmieg

"Sound All Around"
Written by Michael Ritchie

"The Dead Sea Scrolls" show
Introduction by Chris Burda

"The Spirit of the Mummy"
Written by Dan Berkey, J. L. McClure, Richard Rousseau, and Neil Spencer

"Three Angry Scientists"
Written by Melanie Wehrmacher

"Treating Tumors"
Written with Gold by Dr. Lisa Regala

The Missouri History Museum (MHM):
"Shaking Up the Status Quo Scenes from the Civil Rights Movement"
Written by Changa Bey and directed by Alissa Rowan

"Go Home Rosie"
Written by Elizabeth Pickard

"Mrs. Washington Presents Her Compliments"
Written by Elizabeth Pickard

"Getting Dressed: Inside Out in the Corset Age"
Written by Elizabeth Pickard

"In Search of the Mastodon"
Written by Elizabeth Pickard

"St. Louis I Am"
Written by the Teens Make History Players and directed by Elizabeth Pickard

Resources

American Alliance of Museums, http://www.aam-us.org/.

American Association for State and Local History, http://www.aaslh.org/.

Association of Science-Technology Centers, http://www.astc.org/.

Bridal, Tessa. (2004). *Exploring Museum Theatre*. Lanham, MD: AltaMira.

Davis, A. (2013). *Assessing Impact: Igniting the Spark for Science Learning with Museum Theatre*. Berkeley, CA: John F. Kennedy University.

Genoways, Hugh H., editor. (2006). *Museum Philosophy for the Twenty-First Century*. Lanham, MD: AltaMira Press.

Hughes, Catherine. (1998). *Museum Theatre: Communicating with Visitors through Drama*. Portsmouth, NH: Heinemann Drama.

———. (2008). *Performance for Learning: How Emotions Play a Part*. Columbus: Ohio State University Press.

International Museum Theatre Alliance—IMTAL, http://www.imtal.org/.

Magelssen, Scott. (2007). *Living History Museums: Undoing History through Performance*. Lanham, MD: Scarecrow Press.

Widrich, Leo. (2012). "What Listening to a Story Does to Our Brains." Buffer blog. http://blog.bufferapp.com/science-of-storytelling-why-telling-a-story-is-the-most-powerful-way-to-activate-our-brains.

Index

Monterey Bay Aquarium, 21, *36,* 69, 80

Movement in Black and White program (MHM), 35–36

MSI. *See* Museum of Science and Industry, Chicago

museum(s), revolution in, 29–30

museum education, 30

Museum of History and Technology, xiv

Museum of Science and Industry, Chicago (MSI): about, xii–xiii; collaborative design process, 3–4; demonstrations/presentations, *40, 41;* interpreters, 62; interpreter training, 73; museum theatre, 51–52, *52;* program implementation plan, 93; programming approach, 24; tours, 37

Museums for a New Century Commission Report, 29

museum theatre, 48–54; characteristics of, 49–50; collaborative design of spaces for, importance and benefits of, 8; definition of, 49; examples, 50–52, *52, 53;* expectations of, 59; at MHC, 8, 13, *53;* at MHM, 5, 50; at NCM, 22–23, 89–91; power of, 52–54, 54n8; and science learning, 81; script writing for, 77–80; at SMM, xxii, xxivn1, 18, 20, *21;* at SMV, 50, 57, *73;* techniques, 49; vs. traditional theatre, 49–50

Museum without Walls (Atlanta), x

My House to the White House exhibit (NCM), 22

National Children's Museum (NCM): about, xiii; collaborative design at, 5; demonstrations/presentations, 41–42; guest presenters, 37; immersive exhibits, 22–23, *23;* interpreter training, 71; on meetings,

15; program and play list, 105; program development process, 56, 57; theatre company master plan (2011), 89–91

National Museum of American History (NMAH): about, xvii; benefits of collaborative design for, 25, 26; civil rights movement programs, 8, 9–10; Flag Hall programs, 8–10; on history education, 38; interpreters, 61–62; *Join the Student Sit-Ins* program, 10, 25, 51; on live vs. electronic interpretation, 75; museum theatre, 51; object carts, 38; program and play list, 105; program expectations, 59; tours, 36

NCM. *See* National Children's Museum

NCM Theatre Company master plan (2011), 89–91

Night Journey touring exhibit (CMA), 12

NMAH. *See* National Museum of American History

object carts, 38; examples, 12, 38, *39;* History á la Cart program (MHC), 13–14, 38, *39, 85*–87

organization: for collaborative design, 2, 15–16; separating education and public programs, 30

Our Minnesota exhibit (SMM), 11

The Participatory Museum (Simon), 38

performance space. *See* program spaces

Perry, Ivory, 36, 50

personal questions, 69

Philadelphia Zoo, 80

Pickard, Elizabeth: on interpretive programming, 4, 5, 30; on live vs. electronic interpretation, 75; role at MHM, xv, 4, 62

Pioneer Zephyr tour (MSI), 37